Along the Discipleship Road

Text copyright © Jay Colwill 2006
The author asserts the moral right
to be identified as the author of this work

Published by
The Bible Reading Fellowship
First Floor, Elsfield Hall
15–17 Elsfield Way, Oxford OX2 8FG
Website: www.brf.org.uk

ISBN 1 84101 401 X
ISBN-13 978 1 84101 401 2
First published 2006
10 9 8 7 6 5 4 3 2 1 0
All rights reserved

Acknowledgments
Scripture quotations are taken from the Holy Bible, New International
Version, copyright © 1973, 1978, 1984 by International Bible Society,
are used by permission of Hodder & Stoughton Limited. All rights
reserved. 'NIV' is a registered trademark of International Bible Society.
UK trademark number 1448790.

The extract from *Common Worship: Services and Prayers for the Church of
England* is copyright © The Archbishops' Council 2000.
A catalogue record for this book is available from the British Library

Printed in Singapore by Craft Print International Ltd

Following Jesus today

Along the Discipleship Road

Jay Colwill

Thank you
to my parents who started me on the road;
to the churches in Reading, Bracknell and Orpington that
have let me join them on the road;
to my wife, Jo, who tirelessly encourages me on the road.

Dedicated to Lewis and Anna
May you take your next hill, and the next and the next...

Contents

Foreword

This is a sensible and down-to-earth guide about discipleship and how Jesus deals with our 'blockages' in following him, gradually changing us so that we are more and more like him.

As a priest in the Church of England, Jay appeals to its more catholic side in his use of the saints as examples of godly living. His purpose, however, is not just the growth of personal holiness but the building up of the body. There is also an evangelistic aspect to it because the book gives his readers an opportunity to consider the cost of discipleship.

Jay takes us on a 'bicycle ride' through the first century, but the purpose is to help us to live with Jesus now and to be followers of his in the confusing and fast-changing, but also exhilarating, world of the 21st-century.

This book can be profitably read for personal devotion or in groups. It is also a very good aid for those engaged in teaching classes on Bible characters.

+*Michael Nazir-Ali*

The long ride to freedom

Sometimes, I wonder why I bother. There I am at the bottom of the hill, with gravity to fight against. Add to that the weight of the pack on my back as well as my body weight and the weight of the bicycle underneath me. Mountain biking is one of my favourite pastimes. I've always loved the great outdoors and I love to see as much of it as possible. To my mind, walking can be slow and does not cover enough ground. Driving a car is inhibiting and keeps you trapped in a metal bubble. Mountain biking, on the other hand, can provide the dual benefits of enjoying the countryside and doing so at speed. This is not always the case, however. Speed and enjoyment can be severely restricted by many challenging obstacles. As I say, I wonder why I bother!

One particularly memorable experience was day two of a three-day solo mountain bike ride along the 75-mile length of the Ridgeway, one of the most ancient 'roads' in the south of England. It is, in fact, a grassy track that may be used by vehicles in sections. I had decided that I would cycle it as a form of spiritual retreat, stopping off at some of the churches and Christian centres along the way.

On the second day, I found myself on an ascent, making my way up Uffington Hill, known for its famous image of a white horse carved in the chalky soil. It was raining hard, my legs were aching, and I was saddle-sore. I was also about halfway through my ride that day, half-way on my journey, so it would take as long to go back as it would to go forward. Exhaustion was making me reconsider whether this bike ride had been such a good idea. Surely there were easier ways to receive spiritual refreshment? Perhaps I should have thought about the adventure more carefully...

God speaks to me at times like that—not with a voice like thunder, or in any way audibly. He just challenges me: which priorities in my life am I willing to sweat over? Which of the challenges that lie ahead am I prepared to overcome? Am I willing to turn the pedals over and over again in order to take the next hill? More importantly, am I willing to persevere in areas of my life that are more important than mountain biking?

Sometimes, as Christians, we may wonder why we bother. By choosing to follow Jesus, we have (as it were) decided to pick up our mountain bikes, shoulder a backpack of provisions and embark upon an adventure that will challenge us, take us into unknown territory and test our stamina and will. Then, after we have gone so far that there is no turning back, we face yet another hill.

This is a book about some of the hills that we will face. While the Gospels are the best guide to discipleship, and there are many books already available on the the subject, what interests me are the obstacles that can stop us journeying on the discipleship road. Many people begin that journey. They may respond to the gospel through a large mission event, a 'discovering Christianity' course or through a personal invitation to come along to church. Yet, having begun the journey, when they are on the road and confront the first hill, will they face the challenge head-on or turn back?

Fellow strugglers

As I study the Gospel stories, it becomes increasingly clear how much they can teach us. Jesus' calling of his disciples was no casual whim, and, through studying their characters, we can learn about what it means to be a follower of Jesus. The Roman Catholic Church has almost cornered the market on this one! They have looked to the saints of the New Testament for centuries and held them up as examples for living, whereas the Protestant denominations have— almost as a knee-jerk reaction—tended to overlook the individual stories of the disciples in order to focus on the person and work of Jesus Christ, as the only model for us to follow.

While I hold firmly to the view that Jesus Christ is the focus of our prayer and praise, as well as the ultimate example for us to follow, I can't help noticing that Jesus drew real people around him, with all their weaknesses and their faults, in order to shine a light into our lives and say, 'Look, I could meet these people in their situations and provide all that they needed. Don't you think that I can do the same for you?' It is the interaction between Jesus and ordinary, everyday people that makes his teaching, example and sacrifice so compelling. The people with whom he spent the most time, the ones on whom he had the greatest impact, were his disciples.

In his autobiography *God, Where Are You?* Gerard Hughes tells of a recurring picture that he would have as a novice Jesuit priest when asked to meditate. He says: 'I tried to pray, wanted to pray, struggled to keep awake and dispel what were called distractions.' Yet the picture that kept returning was one of him riding a chainless bicycle. He goes on, 'The image was a true reflection of what was going on inside. I was trying to find a God who was separate from everyday experience.'[1]

This image appeals to me on a number of levels. Firstly, I can relate to the bicycle experience! There are many times when, no matter how hard I work, how much energy I put in, something is stopping me from making real progress: the chain has come off, or a tyre has gone flat, or the gears have got 'mashed'. With the frustration levels rising, I have to stop, dismount and cease progress in order to repair any damage or put right any malfunctioning part. Secondly, Hughes' honesty with his readers is helpful because so often we struggle to connect with God through prayer, Bible study, worship or some social activity, but, no matter how determinedly we may 'pedal' our way through the activity, nothing seems to happen.

It took a while for Hughes to recognize that the picture he kept on seeing was God's way of speaking to him. We too can fail to hear what God is trying to tell us, and so fail to see what is stopping us from progressing as disciples.

Big enough to get lost in

One of the most enjoyable aspects of off-road cycling in recent years has resulted from the Forestry Commission opening up large areas of Crown Estate land to the public. This means that there are many parts of England where you can cycle, walk or picnic in densely planted forests. Most have been planted with pines because it is a fast-growing lumber that can be effectively replanted after 'harvesting'. I used to live on the edge of one such forest. It was on the 'fire roads' (tracks left clear for forestry vehicles) that divide one section of forest from another that I caught the bug for off-road cycling. One of the significant problems of off-road cycling in forests, however, is the ease with which you can get lost! The trees are tall, so they hide any landmarks that might help you get your bearings. The tracks and fire roads all look the same, so it is easy to get disorientated. Maps are often inaccurate, and don't show road junctions accurately, or bends curving at just the right angle.

We live in a different kind of forest: a forest of words and meaning. Different generations and cultures endue particular words with particular power, while words that carried great significance in the past have no place in our language today. A word like 'fraternity' might once have been a potent symbol of the uniting interests of a state or nation. Now, such a word is seldom used as a description of community life. In everyday conversation, words like 'sin' have become taboo, or are considered inappropriate or overly judgmental. Other words have taken on a persuasive power of their own. Words like 'community' and 'freedom', 'choice' and 'opportunity' are in vogue and are deployed liberally as argument-winning phrases that can trump your opponent. If you want to prove my point, just try listening to politicians being interviewed on the radio one morning and count how many times they use such key words and phrases. Theologian Richard Bauckham points out that such 'big' words are not always tied down to a definition:

Of course, like other big words, [freedom] can be abused. Its very potency makes it irresistible to every politician and opinion-former. The political rhetoric of freedom may cover a multitude of evils. It may be no more than a slogan among the empty claims and counter-claims of those who compete for power... Freedom is a word that can express the highest idealism and the crassest selfishness. But it has not been totally tarnished by abuse. It still points to something infinitely desirable.[2]

When we are wandering in our own forest of words and meanings, it is easy to lose our way. The maps are usually inadequate and often not to scale; paths may turn right when the map indicates that they go straight on. We can be confused by the choices that confront us if we wish to follow Jesus as a disciple. This is where Jesus' inter-actions with his disciples can teach and guide us. When we are on the downhill slope (like James the apostle, perhaps) what would Jesus' response be? If we are in the mire of dependency (as Mary Magdalene was), what would Jesus say?

Our need for help in the life situations that we face is wonderfully matched by the Bible's ability to provide a framework for living. The disciples' failings are probably mirrored by our own. However many years have passed since their lifetimes, humankind's ability to fall short of God's standards has remained pretty consistent.

Being a disciple

In an often-retold anecdote, a man with a sandwich board walks up and down the street of a major city. On one side of the sandwich board are the words, 'I'm a fool for Jesus'. On the back of the sandwich board is the question, 'Whose fool are you?' The impli-cation of this question is that everyone is 'foolish' for someone or something.

A similar question is posed by Dallas Willard: 'Who teaches you? Whose disciple are you? Honestly. One thing is for sure: You are somebody's disciple. You learned how to live from somebody.'[3] Each of us is guided or influenced by a number of teachers—from our parents to our peer group, through those who taught us at school or college. Then there are the pop stars, sports personalities or trend-setters who influence us through our culture. We are all taught by somebody. We are all somebody's disciple. So what does it mean to be a disciple of Jesus?

Dallas Willard puts it plainly: *'I am with him to learn from him how to be like him.'*[4] Willard amplifies this definition by adding, 'A disciple or apprentice is simply someone who has decided to be with another person, under appropriate conditions, in order to become capable of doing what that person does or to become what that person is.'[5]

As I have already said, the purpose of this book is to examine what it means to 'be with' Jesus today and what barriers might stop us from being with him and learning from him as his disciples. What are the particular pressures faced by 21st-century disciples? As I have suggested, Jesus can help us to answer those questions as we look at the lives of his disciples and, in particular, the way that he interacts with them. This does not mean that we have to go back in time and lead lives that culturally resemble those of men and women in the first century AD. Dallas Willard clarifies the meaning of discipleship by adding: 'I am not learning from [Jesus] how to lead his life. His life on earth was a transcendently wonderful one. But it has now been led. Neither I nor anyone else, even himself, will ever lead it again. And he is, in any case, interested in my life, that very existence that is me.'[6] We are not called to be Jesus, or even to be his first-century followers. We are called to be ourselves, his 21st-century followers, putting the values of God's kingdom at the centre of our lives.

Questions for reflection

1. Whose disciples are you? Who are your main influences?
2. What aspects of our culture do you find morally confusing?
3. As we begin to think about disciples, which New Testament disciple do you know most about? Which one do you relate to most closely?
4. In worship, prayer, social action or Bible study, where do you most often get stuck?

Thomas: sidetracked by doubt

Now Thomas (called Didymus), one of the Twelve, was not with the disciples when Jesus came. So the other disciples told him, 'We have seen the Lord!' But he said to them, 'Unless I see the nail marks in his hands and put my finger where the nails were, and put my hand into his side, I will not believe it.' A week later his disciples were in the house again, and Thomas was with them. Though the doors were locked, Jesus came and stood among them and said, 'Peace be with you!' Then he said to Thomas, 'Put your finger here; see my hands. Reach out your hand and put it into my side. Stop doubting and believe.' Thomas said to him, 'My Lord and my God!' Then Jesus told him, 'Because you have seen me, you have believed; blessed are those who have not seen and yet have believed.'

JOHN 20:24–29

Doubt is a human experience that touches us all. Ian Hislop, the editor of *Private Eye* and regular on the TV show *Have I Got News for You*, wrote this a few years ago.

At the age I am now, Jesus' life was finished. He had either completed an extraordinary mission or had been pointlessly and tragically executed. The end is either Christ's last cry of desolation in Luke: 'My God, my God, why have you forsaken me?' or it is the certainty of the words, 'Father, into your hands, I commit my spirit.' I don't know. I've sat in churches thinking this is all rubbish. I've thought the mockers' thoughts. And, at other times, I have felt that this is all there is. I don't know. I don't know.[7]

14

Hislop candidly expresses his doubts—and his faith. Like him, many of us have times of real questioning. For each of us, there are days when we are ready to walk with Jesus down the road, wherever he takes us. On other days, uncertainty creeps in, and we wonder whether we can take a single step.

A famous TV show of the late 1990s was *The X Files*, with its slogan 'The truth is out there'. But some people doubt that they can hope to find the truth. Others are not sure whether there is any truth to find. These feelings have been magnified in recent decades, as our culture has gone through rapid changes. In the decades after World War II, certainties of good and evil seem to have disappeared. Certainties about personal morality are now being challenged, so that adults and children alike wonder what is right and wrong. All these influences lead thinkers to ask whether there is any measurement of truth that can be made. Many argue that moral standards do not exist independently from our own personal preferences. If the general assumption is that truth cannot be measured, then our society exerts a pressure upon anyone who makes truth claims or holds on to absolutes to provide a framework for living. This pressure involves mocking any group who suggests that their position is based upon spiritual revelation or founded upon long-standing historical practices. Their position can then be criticized as being outmoded and arcane.

For Christians who affirm a belief that Jesus is 'the way and the truth and the life (John 14:6), this immediately raises a tension in their own lives, because of the need to hold together a life of faith in God with a world that constantly questions and challenges. If we do not work to understand this tension and how we live with it, we can be led off the discipleship track and on to a byway of doubt.

Defining doubt

Doubt means being in two minds, having a divided judgment when facing two choices, wavering in decision. A byway is sometimes defined as a secondary or side road. You usually meet them at a fork in the road. Sometimes the way ahead is clear, but more often than not, it is indistinct. If we take the wrong path, we may find ourselves sidetracked and diverted from the goal of our journey. Our doubts can be like this. We may doubt that God has the character to keep his promises. We may doubt that the traditions or creeds of the church reveal anything meaningful about the nature of God. These doubts may be based upon our understanding of revelation from God. Other doubts may be based upon whether or not we feel God loves us and is close to us.

Since I am a Christian who makes a living from talking to people about faith, people are very interested in finding out whether I doubt. I am often asked if I ever question my beliefs in God. Because the questioner doesn't always tell me why they are asking, I have to guess. Is it because my doubting God's desire for relationship will reassure them that it's OK to doubt too? Will they feel more comfortable in their own unbelief because they know that the vicar finds it hard to believe everything? Whatever their motive, I try to be honest and own up to my own doubts, both large and small.

The focus of that doubt can have its source in questions thrown up by the apparent contradiction between God's word and our human experience. Doubt may also imply a desire to know more. In that respect, it can be positive. Many of us will have echoed the words of the father of an epileptic son, who came to Jesus and said, 'I do believe; help me overcome my unbelief!' (Mark 9:24). Here, doubt can be a passing phase as we move towards faith, seeking understanding.[8]

Thus far, in my spiritual journey, I have not encountered what some call the 'dark night of the soul', when God seems so absent that it is as if he is no longer real, loving or relevant. That day may come, though, so in thinking about faith and doubt, in some small way I may be better prepared to face up to it.

The skeleton in the closet of faith

Jesus' encounters with his disciples in the Gospels demonstrate how he lovingly encourages them to move from unbelief to belief, from misunderstanding to understanding and from doubt to faith. As circumstances arise that lead us to question our faith, we can turn to Jesus' words of correction, rebuke, encouragement and training. They can speak to us today. We can place ourselves in the company of his disciples; we can step into their shoes and walk with Jesus down the road, or talk to him in the locked room (John 20:26). There, he can speak into our situation as he spoke into theirs; he can touch our lives as he transformed theirs.

Thomas is the one disciple who is known for his doubt. It is possible that more people outside the church know of 'Doubting Thomas' than of Simon Peter. In thinking about the whole issue of doubt, it is worth stating the obvious: faith in Jesus Christ is rarely a straightforward affair. Sometimes the gap between doubt and faith can be very small.

The great men and women of faith, whom we remember only for their spiritual strength, were sometimes racked with doubt. The great church reformer Martin Luther battled with doubt and depression. 'For more than a week,' he once wrote, 'Christ was wholly lost. I was shaken by desperation and blasphemy against God.'[9] English mystic Evelyn Underhill admitted to times when the 'whole spiritual scheme seems in question'.[10] Yet there are some common ingredients to doubt, illustrated in Thomas's life, that can help us understand our own doubts. In the words of Philip Yancey, 'Doubt is the skeleton in the closet of faith, and I know no better way to treat a skeleton than to bring it into the open and expose it for what it is: not something to hide or fear, but a hard structure on which living tissue may grow.'[11] As we examine the life of Thomas and his interaction with Jesus, we can put flesh on the bones of our doubt.

Factors affecting faith

The first factor that can affect faith is personality.[12] We have only glimpses of Thomas's character elsewhere in the Gospels. In John 11:16, he shows his loyalty where Jesus goes up to Jerusalem in the face of great opposition: 'Then Thomas (called Didymus) said to the rest of the disciples, "Let us also go, that we may die with him." While it is possible to see this as an example of courage and faithfulness to Jesus' call, it could also indicate that Thomas was a gloomy, rather pessimistic person. Did he struggle all along with the amazing and positive claims of Jesus to be the Son of God, the Messiah? In this respect, Thomas is a very human character in the story, one with whom we can identify. It might seem to us—or to those whom we know—that the good news of Jesus is too wonderful to be true. It may seem impossible to believe that one man can forgive sins and bring us back to God. Like Thomas, we may feel more pessimistic than optimistic about our faith in God. The 'happy ever after' ending that we read about, or hear about in the lives of others, may be true for them, but it does not seem likely in our own lives.

Thomas' personality also leads him to be something of a literalist. In John 14:4–5, Jesus says to the disciples, 'You know the way to the place where I am going.' Thomas answers, 'Lord, we don't know where you are going, so how can we know the way?' Jesus was talking of a spiritual journey, but Thomas understood it as a literal one. He lacked spiritual perception, which meant that he found it hard to see beyond the concrete facts of a situation to the reality that Jesus was speaking about. In the locked room in Jerusalem, after Jesus has risen, Thomas takes that literalism to its natural conclusion: 'Unless I see the nail marks in his hands and put my finger where the nails were, and put my hand into his side, I will not believe it' (John 20:25).

Understanding personality

Much work has been done over recent decades in identifying the impact that personality has upon faith. One of the most widely used tools for analysing personality and how it affects behaviour is the Myers Briggs Type Indicator™. It suggests that our behaviour is the result of how we receive information about the world (perception) and how we reach decisions based on that information (judgment). In the process of taking in information, we make a series of choices. The Myers Briggs Type Indicator™ suggests that some of us are more inclined to use our five senses (touch, taste, sight, hearing smell) to do this, while others prefer to use what might be called a 'sixth sense'—intuition, feelings or hunches.

Once we have assessed a situation, we go on to make a judgment about it. For some of us, this judgment may be based upon a propensity to use our thinking function. In other words, we decide about things in an impersonal way, based upon a series of personal principles. Others will be inclined to use feelings rather than impersonal criteria for decision making. This means that they will make judgments based upon likes and dislikes, using a more subjective system of values, which also take into account the impact of decisions on others.

The final part of this personality theory suggests where we are likely to go to find energy for daily life. Some are inclined to look outside themselves for this energy, looking to other people and activities to help them recharge their batteries. The Myers Briggs Type Indicator™ describes such people as extraverts. Introverts, on the other hand, are those who find energy from the inner world of abstract ideas and thoughts. Unlike the extravert, introverts can feel daunted by too much stimulus from other people.

If we consider Thomas, what can we learn from the evidence in the New Testament about how his personality leads him to doubt? As we have just seen, our behaviour is the result of how we receive information about the world (perception) and how we reach decisions based on that information (judgment). Doubt arises in our mind when we cannot reconcile the information with our impression of it. In their book *Knowing Me, Knowing You*, Goldsmith and Wharton state:

A Judging attitude towards the world is one that seeks structure, order and control, whilst a Perceiving attitude towards the world prefers to remain open and flexible and is rather more passive than the Judging attitude... Judgers tend to like to have things ordered, whether it be doctrine or liturgy... They have discovered that structure carries them through times of barrenness, and there is a sense of loyalty to the pattern that has been built up. Judgers are less likely to be influenced by the charismatic movement, and are more likely to find succour in traditional forms of worship, discipline and Bible study. [13]

This suggests that Thomas' judging personality was one trait in his life that led him to doubt. He is loyal: 'Let us also go, that we may die with him'. He is structured and recognizes the implications of Jesus' words when they seem to be lost upon the other disciples. When his ordered way of life, following Jesus Christ, is shattered by the events of Good Friday and Easter Day, he seems unable to come to terms with the dramatic power of God's Spirit in raising Christ to life. His ordered mind cannot allow for such a shocking eventuality.

For Thomas, the agonizing tension of doubt develops when his personality struggles to reconcile discipline and orderliness with the world-shaking work of God in raising Jesus to life. But this does not mean that Judgers are the only types who doubt! Perceivers can end up doubting if they feel that God's activity seems to go against their naturally spontaneous and unstructured approach to getting things done. For example, a 'wait and see' attitude to life makes such a person uneasy about making decisions of faith, which in turn can paralyse that person with doubt.

It is worth pausing at this point to reflect on how personality can have a marked impact on our tendency to doubt, no matter what 'type' we are. Are you naturally cautious in life, only wanting to believe in what you can see? Are you susceptible to doubting anything that crops up above and beyond 'the way life is', or, on the other hand, do you view any kind of formal ordering with suspicion? It may be important to focus upon the 'opposite' side of your personality to help you develop a more rounded view of faith in God. For example, a Judging personality, who sees the activity of God as predictable and structured, might struggle with the spontaneous and creative movement of the Holy Spirit as it is seen in the Acts of the Apostles. They might also contest the surprising work of God in their lives and in the lives of others (as testified to in areas of spiritual renewal in parts of the world today). A Perceptive personality, on the other hand, might wrestle with the need for structure and order in their spiritual life. They may find great difficulty in setting aside time for God through prayer, Bible study and solitude. Thus, each personality type might need to consider their corresponding weakness and develop it in order to overcome the extent that it causes them to doubt.

The lone disciple

A second factor that can lead to doubt is isolation: 'Now Thomas (called Didymus), one of the Twelve, was not with the disciples when Jesus came' (v. 24). At this point in the post-Easter story, Thomas has cut himself off from the disciple community. We don't know why. Possibly, he wanted to work through the problems thrown up by the death of Jesus on his own. Perhaps he felt that he could no longer identify with the disciples and what they represented. Whatever the reason, his absence meant that he was penalized by a further week of agonizing struggle. In being isolated, Thomas missed the opportunity of hearing Jesus' words of peace and seeing his risen Saviour. The other disciples were overjoyed at his presence (John 20:20); Thomas was not.

There are many kinds of isolation, all of which can accentuate doubt. As with Thomas, our isolation may be a physical separation from others in our Christian community. Alternatively, it may be a separation from the past, expressed through a cultural rootlessness.[14] (Increasingly, people born in the late 1960s or 1970s can feel a sense of detachment from their national history. This in turn can lead to a breakdown in community and an increase in human isolation, which even technological substitutes such as the Internet cannot mend.) Then again, we may feel isolated from God because of unconfessed sin in our lives. There may be as many reasons to detach ourselves from our community as there are people. In order to simplify these reasons, we shall divide them into three types.

One main reason for increased isolation is the prevailing influence of individualism within our culture. 'We're too busy to have any community spirit,' ran a headline in a local paper. Many popular novels of our time, such as *About a Boy* by Nick Hornby, and *Bridget Jones's Diary* by Helen Fielding, have articulated this sense of detachment from others. The attitude is not unique to secular communities: 'Individualism manifests itself in church life when people start to believe that their own needs are of far greater importance than the Christian community to which they belong.'[15] Our culture's individualistic ideology puts strain upon our innate desire for deep relationships with other human beings, yet people often express a longing for greater community without acknowledging a willingness to submit some of their individual freedoms to the needs of the group.

The second reason for increased isolation among Christians is the failure of the church to function as true community. Jesus prayed for his disciples saying, 'Holy Father, protect them by the power of your name—the name you gave me—so that they may be one as we are one' (John 17:11). Gilbert Bilezikian points out that oneness in community and in faith did express itself in the life of the early church after the time of Pentecost, yet, 'as the effect of that impact wore off and Christians increasingly took for granted both the Holy Spirit and their oneness, the churches had to be constantly reminded of their true identity as the communities of oneness.'[16] The weaknesses and failings of the early church are replicated year by year, decade by decade, up to the present day. This, however, does not negate the centrality of Christian community in inspiring individuals to listen to God, to serve Christ, and to work out their faith in the world. As we have argued, the cultural value of individualism is perhaps stronger now than it was in the time of Thomas. Therefore, each community needs to strive to provide a counter-cultural witness that is more attractive than the consumer-led society in which we live.

The third reason for people's isolation can be a particular life event or circumstance. Much research has been carried out in the last few years identifying people's reasons and motivations for leaving church.[17] The comment of one person at a church where I have served illustrates this point:

I used to be involved in church on a number of different levels. Over time, I went less, and didn't feel missed. Time went on, and I didn't feel that I missed church. I didn't feel that I would be true to myself if I continued to go, even though that relationship with church had once been very important.[18]

Any of these three factors, individually or together, can lead to an increased sense of isolation. When we doubt, we question the depth of our faith. Does it sustain us at the most difficult times? Does it help us to answer life's most pressing questions? Like the Roman commander who oversaw the sacking of Jerusalem and entered the holy of holies, only to find it empty, some of our Christian friends come to examine the core of their faith and find nothing there. For a while, as Derek Tidball writes, 'the outward rituals are maintained and they remain involved in church where, since appearances can be deceptive, many regard them as convinced believers'.[19] But when the changes and chances of life, or some other factor, affect them, they leave the Christian community. Derek Tidball suggests that doubt may be present in the believer in spite of attendance at public worship, particularly when it is nominal and merely routine.

In today's world, it takes commitment to meet together, whether in our small groups or at church on a Sunday. Being isolated from other Christians is easier than being with them when we live busier and more fragmented lives. To attend church on a Sunday morning, we have to let our spouse know we're going, or persuade our children to join us. We'll have to organize our Sunday lunch so that it isn't burnt or frozen on our return. And when we arrive, we may sit there and think, 'Is God really going to speak to me?' But maybe in a prayer, or a song, maybe in a Bible reading or a talk, it's as if God comes from heaven, sits down and speaks only to us. In a small but significant way, our faith grows, and doubt diminishes.

Thomas came back on track and back into community, and it had an enormous impact. Like him, we can hold on to that promise: 'For where two or three come together in my name, there am I with them' (Matthew 18:20).

Confrontation in faith and doubt

The third factor that led to Thomas' doubt was the sheer contradiction between the cross and the resurrection. Not even the clear and persistent teaching of Jesus could prepare him for it: 'He then began to teach them that the Son of Man must suffer many things and be rejected by the elders, chief priests and teachers of the law, and that he must be killed and after three days rise again. He spoke plainly about this' (Mark 8:31–32a). We read in Luke 18:31–34:

Jesus took the Twelve aside and told them, 'We are going up to Jerusalem, and everything that is written by the prophets about the Son of Man will be fulfilled. He will be turned over to the Gentiles. They will mock him, insult him, spit on him, flog him and kill him. On the third day he will rise again.' The disciples did not understand any of this. Its meaning was hidden from them, and they did not know what he was talking about.

Not even the exuberant testimony of the other disciples after the resurrection could persuade him of it. It contradicted everything he knew, or thought he knew about. He may have expected that Jesus would inaugurate a human kingdom. Perhaps he thought that the resurrection of Jesus was just a figure of speech.

In the course of my ministerial work, I talk to quite a few men in their 20s, 30s and 40s about questions of faith. Time and again, I find that there is one barrier that they can't seem to overcome. They can't understand why Jesus should die for their sin. Their argument is that they are responsible for themselves. After all, they are adult males. They've had to pay for a house, fight their way up the employment ladder, hold positions of influence and authority. Why can't they pay for their own sin as well? They find it tremendously difficult to accept the amazing offer of God to pay for our sin through Jesus and his death on the cross. It seems to contradict everything they thought they understood about life, and so they refuse to believe it, along with doubting Thomas.

What these men are going through is a reconsideration of their worldview. As Tom Wright says, 'Worldview, in fact, embraces all deep-level human perceptions of reality.'[20] Of course, they won't describe the process as such (most of us wouldn't), but their intellectual reappraisal of life has already begun. For Thomas, his worldview was challenged not by the crucifixion of Jesus but by the resurrection of Jesus. That one event threw his mind into turmoil as he tried to reconcile it with his own human experience—dead people don't usually come to life again. Although he would have witnessed the raising of Lazarus (we read about this in John 11:38–44), he may have considered it to have been a resuscitation. Because he was not present at Lazarus' death, he may not have been convinced of its finality.

After the resurrection, the other disciples were speaking to Thomas from another ideological universe with their news of extraordinary events—a universe where saviours suffer and dead men rise on the third day. Thomas had to consider his version of reality against theirs, questioning the very foundation from which he answered the fundamental questions of life. What is reality? What is the nature of the world around us? What does it mean to be human? What happens to a person at death? How is it possible to know anything at all? Not surprisingly, the bodily resurrection of Jesus throws into doubt any answers to those questions established before Easter morning. Accordingly, Thomas ends up in crisis.

When he finally does come face to face with the risen Jesus (John 20:24–31), Thomas faces three possible responses.

- He can maintain his pre-Easter worldview, continuing to think that men who are pierced in the heart with a spear (John 19:34) stay dead.
- He can remain in a place of terrible uncertainty and turmoil.
- He can adapt his worldview to incorporate the new reality, the fact that Jesus has indeed risen from the dead.

Doubt, for each one of us, is that place of uncertainty and turmoil. We may express it in specific ways: 'Unless I see the nail marks in his hands and put my finger where the nails were, and put my hand into his side, I will not believe it' (John 20:25). We may be more circumspect in our pronouncements: 'I'm not sure; I don't know any more.' Either way, moving to a position of faith will involve adjusting our view of reality in some way.

Adjusting our view of reality does not mean ignoring life's struggles, however. The 'Christian life' mirrors what we might call our 'everyday life' in that it can be both joy-filled and difficult. This is because our salvation in Jesus is both present and yet to come. If we misunderstand this important balance, we open ourselves to fear and doubt through a misapprehension of our walk with God. We can become disillusioned by the stuggles that we face, because we think that they should be 'miraculously' overcome. In fact, the struggle may be part of the transformational process (theologians call it 'sanctification') that God wants us to go through in order to grow more like Christ. It may also be that the difficulty of the present helps to keep our eyes upon a future that is yet to come.

For one person, the journey from doubt to faith came through an invitation. Over a conversation in an art studio, my (now) wife was asked what she thought about God. Yes, she said, she had gone to church as a child, but the language of the services and the way in which church, and Christianity, seemed so separate from the 'real' world had put her right off. An invitation was made to attend a different kind of Christian gathering. There she experienced language that she could understand and relate to, combined with teaching that made sense to her. Over a period of time, the impact of her reawakened faith caused her to change her degree course, change her career path and develop many new friends and a whole new worldview. Along the way, she met me and our lives changed direction again. I am very thankful for that conversation in the art studio, which caused someone to question the basis for her doubts and offered the opportunity of faith.

Jesus and doubt

To summarize, there are three key factors that can lead us to doubt: our personality, our isolation and the way that our understanding of the Christian faith seems to contradict our experience of life. It may be that we can also identify other factors that lead us personally to doubt.

The most amazing part of Thomas' story of doubt is not Thomas, however. It is Jesus who comes to Thomas in his moment of doubt. Jesus didn't ignore Thomas' personality. The second post-resurrection appearance that Jesus makes is essentially for Thomas' benefit, saying, 'Go on, then, Thomas. You need to know by touching—so go ahead and touch me.' He demonstrates knowledge of the very detail of Thomas' doubt. And he doesn't come to Thomas in a moment of isolation, as doubt could return later ('Did that really happen? Was I dreaming?'). Instead, he comes to him while he is gathered with the other disciples again, thus reinforcing the value of shared revelation and faith. Finally,

Jesus goes to the very heart of Thomas' framework of belief and challenges it by inviting him to place his hands in the nail marks, bringing him through the crisis and into a new place of belief.

As Jesus knew Thomas and his personal struggles in faith, so he knows ours, too. He doesn't reject us, but he comes to us, inviting us to put our faith in a saviour who transforms life. At the same time, Jesus' words to Thomas carry a challenge: 'Stop doubting and believe' (John 20:27). As Jesus meets with us—in a worship song, in a word in the Bible, in a prayer, through the friendship of another Christian—he says to you and to me, 'Stop doubting and believe.' The transformation of Thomas' life was immense. Not only did he serve the church in Jerusalem and Judea, but there is also historical evidence that his mission led him to evangelize and establish the early church in South India.[21] From being 'Doubting Thomas', this disciple becomes an example to us of faith and commitment. He stops being sidetracked by doubt and demonstrates his commit-ment to 'the Way' (Acts 24:14). Jesus lovingly comes and stands before each one of us, in our faith and in our doubt. We stand where Thomas stood, hesitating to move into a deeper relationship. And Thomas' words can be our words—'My Lord and my God!' (John 20:28)—marking a new beginning for him and for us.

Questions for reflection

1. Can you remember a time when you doubted your faith in Jesus Christ? Why did it happen?
2. Are you structured and orderly, or spontaneous and unstructured?
3. Jesus knows our faith and doubt better than we know ourselves. What do you need to say to him right now?

2

Andrew's opportunity to overcome the obstacles

The next day John was there again with two of his disciples. When he saw Jesus passing by, he said, 'Look, the Lamb of God!' When the two disciples heard him say this, they followed Jesus. Turning around, Jesus saw them following and asked, 'What do you want?' They said, 'Rabbi' (which means Teacher), 'where are you staying?' 'Come,' he replied, 'and you will see.' So they went and saw where he was staying, and spent that day with him. It was about the tenth hour. Andrew, Simon Peter's brother, was one of the two who heard what John had said and who had followed Jesus. The first thing Andrew did was to find his brother Simon and tell him, 'We have found the Messiah' (that is, the Christ). And he brought him to Jesus. Jesus looked at him and said, 'You are Simon son of John. You will be called Cephas' (which, when translated, is Peter).

JOHN 1:35–42

'Opportunity' is a feel-good word. It paints a picture for me of wide horizons and limitless possibilities. Many other words are equally loaded with emotion. When you say them or think them, they instantly generate an emotional response, either positive or negative. Words such as 'tolerance' are generally considered to be positive words because of the attitudes that lie behind them. ('Intolerance' is not something that people will gladly own up to, and we've even invented the phrase 'zero tolerance' to get around the problem of using the negative form!) Another powerful word is 'freedom', with its ability to inspire dedication and self-sacrifice. Most people know that it is something to which they should aspire, although of course one individual's freedom can lead to another's oppression.

Words do not only have a meaning; they have a history and a context that also evoke a response in us, either positive or negative. Within English culture, one of the most renowned changes of meaning is in the word 'gay'. The history and context of that word have changed quite significantly over the decades. Other words, which might have been used to refer to someone's disability, would now be seen as offensive and inappropriate. (Someone with cerebral palsy would consider it an insult to be called a 'spastic', for example.)

As I mentioned at the start of the chapter, 'opportunity' is a word with a positive feel. It means 'a favourable, appropriate or advantageous combination of circumstances'.[22] Like 'freedom', it is full of promise. Historically, the popularity of the word, at least in part, comes from the ideal of the American dream, evoking a land of wide horizons, where I can satisfy my desire 'to do what I want with my life, unrestricted by social expectations, responsibilities to others, class structures, economic pressures or whatever'.[23] Because of the American cultural dominance of the last century, we in the UK have also embraced this ideal of 'opportunity'. In more recent times, the word has gained resonance in a post-Thatcherite understanding of freedom and choice. Today, we live in a culture seduced by a dream of opportunity that can in some way be bought and sold —a society where everything is described in terms of 'consumers' and 'choice'. The individual strives to become who he or she wants to be by buying the right clothes, driving the right car, or having the right job.

To get a handle on the opportunities that are presented to us, I thought I would find out how many 'opportunities' are out there for me to take, using the Google Internet search engine. Narrowing my search a little, I typed in the words 'opportunity to help others', which brought up 19,300,000 opportunities to consider! In the UK alone, there are 2,260,000 opportunities listed in the areas of caring, helping and voluntary service.[24] You name it, someone is offering you an opportunity in it. Or take a look at the small ads in your local free newspaper. The fact is, we are not short of opportunities of any kind. What is the case, however, is that we are short of the right opportunities to know life in all its fullness. This is where Andrew made the right choice.

Opportunity knocks

Andrew is not a larger-than-life character in the New Testament. In fact, he doesn't have a high profile at all. He is most famous as the brother of Peter, and he very much stands in Peter's shadow. He is, if you like, the patron saint of younger brothers (as well as being the patron saint of Scotland, fishermen, Greece and Russia). The description of Andrew as 'Simon Peter's brother' is the fate of many younger siblings, identified only in relation to their older and more prominent family member. It is not always easy to be the younger brother of an outspoken and extravert leader, but, in our reading at the start of this chapter, and throughout the Gospels, Andrew makes a very important mark upon the life of the church.

The name Andrew means 'manly', and it may have been a nickname given to him, much as Simon was given the name Peter, 'the rock'. As a labourer and fisherman, he may have had the physique to match the name. Although we don't know much about him, we do know that he was first a follower of John the Baptist. Not all of John's followers became disciples of Jesus. (Acts 19:1–6 tells us that some people remained disciples of John even after his death.) Neither do the Gospels state explicitly that John expected his disciples to transfer their allegiance to Christ. Because of the teaching of John, however, we can surmise that he saw himself as a forerunner to the Messiah. From this, we can assume that just as he would have passed on the role of proclaiming God's message, so would he have passed on his disciples to aid in the work. We don't get the impression that these Baptist disciples were scurrilously running off to follow another, while abandoning their true master; quite the contrary, in fact. They were being true to his teaching and to his perception of his own role: 'The friend who attends the bridegroom waits and listens for him, and is full of joy when he hears the bridegroom's voice. That joy is mine, and it is now complete. He must become greater; I must become less' (John 3:29–30).

So the fisherman and follower of John the Baptist decides to leave his nets and take up full-time with Jesus. As 21st-century people, brought up on 'therapy speak' and novels that delve into the inner psyche of their characters, we may feel a bit frustrated at this point. How does Andrew make the switch from Baptist to Messiah? How does he 'feel' about it? What tension does he experience between home and previous career and the new life of full-time disciple and evangelist? All of these questions may be legitimate, but the Gospels are not interested in answering them. The transition of Andrew and the other fishermen from one role to another is something that the Gospel writers touch on only lightly (Mark 1:16–18 and John 1:40–41). Despite the paucity of information, though, we can glimpse the sense of opportunism in Andrew already. John the Baptist only needed to mention that Jesus was 'the Lamb of God' on two occasions (John 1:29, 36) for Andrew to grasp its significance and follow Christ. Other Baptist disciples would need encouragement from a third party, such as another follower, and some simply failed to understand that John the Baptist was the forerunner to Christ at all. Andrew needed no further prompting.

'What do you want?'

Have you ever tried to get the attention of someone special or important? It can be a daunting prospect. I remember standing patiently waiting to meet the former England rugby player, Martin

Bayfield, so that I could get his autograph. He is about 6 feet 10 inches tall, and a mountain of a man, who played the 'body double' for Hagrid in the *Harry Potter* films. (I was getting the autograph for my two children, honest!) As I waited, I felt rather insignificant and unimportant, and when my turn came, I probably burbled out my request. He was very gracious, though, and I got my autograph!

Andrew and another unnamed disciple went to meet Jesus. We might not describe Jesus as famous at that time, but he certainly would have been renowned in the circles in which Andrew moved. John had identified him as the Messiah, and Andrew would have acted respectfully in his presence. The conversation that took place was so true to life. Like my encounter, there seems to be a little bit of trepidation in Andrew's footsteps. For Jesus to have the opportunity to speak first, Andrew must have been somewhat 'backward in coming forward'. Before he could begin to frame a question, Jesus turned around and asked, 'What do you want?' (John 1:38).

The Gospel writer implies that Jesus was referring to a deeper question, not just Andrew's immediate need for that day. He was really asking Andrew—as well as the first Gospel readers, and even you and me—what we want from life. Underneath it all, what do you really want? If you are a high achiever, climbing up the career ladder, one day you will run out of rungs. What do you want? If you are a low achiever, and you are running out of hope, what do you want? If you are old and are running out of time, or young and running out of alternatives, what do you want?

People today are more rootless than previous generations were. We tend to be detached from our past, forgetful or dismissive of the questions and struggles of our forebears. We may assume that we are the first to feel this uncertainty and sense of flux. We cover our sense of disconnectedness with virtual communities, virtual realities, ecstasy that comes in pill form, and TV shows where we watch people sleep when we cannot. All of this is overlaid with busyness—in work, in family life, and in play. There is a bewildering amount of choice. (Supermarkets stock 64 different varieties of breakfast cereals alone.) Then we are told in adverts and in 'makeover' shows what we should desire or buy. We don't always make the time to ask ourselves what we want.

The writer of this psalm had a very different agenda:

> *Hear my prayer, O Lord God Almighty;*
> *listen to me, O God of Jacob.*
> *Look upon our shield, O God;*
> *look with favour on your anointed one.*
> *Better is one day in your courts*
> *than a thousand elsewhere;*
> *I would rather be a doorkeeper in the house of my God*
> *than dwell in the tents of the wicked.*
> *For the Lord God is a sun and shield;*
> *the Lord bestows favour and honour;*
> *no good thing does he withhold*
> *from those whose walk is blameless.*
> *O Lord Almighty,*
> *blessed is the man who trusts in you.*
> PSALM 84:8–12

'What do you want?' is an important question, but it is most completely answered by a relationship rather than by a reply. The psalmist wanted more than anything else to be in the presence of God. This is what Jesus offered to Andrew, and what he offers to you and me today.

The disciples' response to Jesus' question was a simple one. 'They said, "Rabbi" (which means Teacher), "where are you staying?"' (v. 38). The term 'Rabbi' was used in Jesus' day as a term of respect for anyone who was considered to be an important teacher. (Only later would it refer to someone who had gone through an appropriate course in rabbinical instruction.) Andrew uses this term, which literally means 'my great one'. Perhaps he felt something of the awesome presence of a 'big man'.

Jesus' response was also a simple one. 'Come… and you will see'

(v. 39). There is a special feeling in being welcomed by someone 'important'. People speak of the privilege of being invited to one of the Queen's garden parties, or having a backstage pass to a concert of one of their favourite bands. Andrew must have felt something of these emotions. Perhaps he hadn't expected such an immediate and warm response.

'To be or not to be'

The first and greatest opportunity that Andrew took was to be with Jesus, thus setting an example of committed discipleship for us. The first rule of discipleship is to go where Jesus is—and stay there. Don't worry too much about what you should contribute to the relationship, but just take time to be with him. This is much easier to do when Jesus is there in the flesh, of course. What on earth does 'being with Jesus' mean for us? In what way is it an opportunity that we can grasp? While so many contemporary worship songs call us to 'draw close' and 'come into a greater intimacy with Christ',[25] we need to find out where Jesus is in order to start exploring the intimate relationship that he offers.

Where is Jesus today, so that we can be with him? We have already considered the importance of community in helping us to over-come doubts and uncertainty in our faith journey. The Christian community—whether in the form of a small group or church congregation—is the primary place where we can meet Jesus. Why? Because when we are there, we will hear his words as we read the Bible. We will hear others talk to him in prayer, and, through listening to them, we will begin to learn our own mode of conversation with Jesus. He will speak to us in the teaching of others, as the Holy Spirit communicates through their words. In worship, whether spoken or sung, we can tell Jesus how we feel about him. In prayers of confession, through receiving Holy Communion, we can tell Jesus how we feel about ourselves. Whether in moments of stillness or in noisy celebration, in a front room or in a big church, the Christian community provides a vital place where we can experience the presence of Jesus.

The hurried life

What about spending more time with Jesus, day by day? That was Andrew's privilege, as he was able to follow Jesus through the Judean countryside, listening to his teaching and seeing his miracles. Jesus ushered in the very kingdom of God in Andrew's presence. In the first four chapters of John's Gospel, we read that he called people to follow him, carried out miracles (changing water into wine), got angry (in the cleansing of the temple) and broke down social barriers (by speaking to a Samaritan woman at a well).

How can we make Andrew's experience our own? In today's world, it seems increasingly difficult to find moments when we can experience real relationship with Christ. Even if we have a routine of a daily 'quiet time' involving prayer, Bible study and reflection, this can become yet another item on the 'to do' list that needs completing before we move on to the next task. If I'm honest, some of my prayer times are not very quiet at all. They are full of 'white noise', the distractions of hundreds of other jobs and other thoughts. What Andrew enjoyed was a deeper experience, which involved seeing Jesus change society and the lives of individuals.

Before engaging in all this kingdom activity, however, Jesus and his disciples had times of quietness together. (Mark's Gospel emphasizes this in the early days of Jesus' ministry in particular.) What I know I need to seek—and it may be true for you as well— is a time with Jesus that is about silent companionship. Tom Wright puts it this way: 'Silence is the gentle kiss that tell us it's all right to relax now… Silence is the sense of calm when all the tears have been cried.'[26] We all need a greater sense of stillness in our meetings with Jesus.

John Ortberg tells how he phoned a friend of his who gave good spiritual counsel, to ask him for advice. The man paused for a moment on the phone and then said, 'You must ruthlessly eliminate "hurry" from your life.' Ortberg waited for the man to say more, but he remained silent. 'I've got that one written down. What's the next point?' he said. 'That's all,' the man replied. 'You must ruthlessly eliminate "hurry" from your life.'[27] Most of us live hurried lives. Not just busy lives—which can be a good thing—but hurried lives. As I was writing these words, a woman came to my door to speak to me. She was expecting to book an appointment because she thought that I was too busy. I could have got my diary out and put her off, yet, was I really so busy that I couldn't see her there and then? So I asked her in, and I was thankful that we spent time together, talking and coming to understand one another better. Andrew took the opportunity to 'down tools' and spend time with Jesus. He left the hurry and pressure of his previous life and found a new purpose as a disciple. Being with Jesus, we can do the same.

Many people find that they can spend time with Jesus and eliminate the hurry by simply letting him join them on a walk or a ride. We can specifically include him in our conversations and acknowledge his presence on our journey. If I feel 'driven' in my times of prayer and Bible reading, I have found it helpful to take a break from my regular pattern and just sit in stillness. That way, I can include Jesus in my thinking and seek his wisdom for my decision. Many people write down prayers, and I also write down my spiritual conversations at these times. For me, such periods of unstructured prayer send me back refreshed into the patterns that I have so benefited from over the years. I can then use them again to communicate effectively with God.

Telling others

It is only after we have spent 'quality time' with Jesus that we start to perceive the true value of the relationship. As a result of his encounter, Andrew seized a second opportunity in the space of just 24 hours: 'The first thing Andrew did was to find his brother Simon and tell him, "We have found the Messiah" (that is, the Christ)' (v. 41). It is through his powerful encounter with Jesus that Andrew gets fired up to share his discovery. It is through powerful encounters with Jesus that we too can become fired up to tell others about him. Whether we meet Jesus through personal Bible study and reflection, attending a church service, or simply through reading a book, if we are excited about the encounter and it has transformed our lives in some way, we don't keep it to ourselves but tell someone else about it. Preferably, we tell someone like Andrew's brother Peter, who hasn't had the opportunity to meet Jesus personally yet.

Let's pause for a moment, and ask ourselves a question: how many people do we know who are not Christians? How many of our friends do not believe in Christ? What tends to happen is that the longer we are Christians, the more Christian friends we have, and the fewer friends we have who are non-believers. This is partly because a shared relationship in Christ makes the friendship much more meaningful, and partly because we naturally gravitate towards like-minded people, such as other Christians who share our values and worldview. In some ways, this is a good thing. Such people provide much-needed spiritual, emotional and practical support. At the same time, however, it is just as important that we consciously form and maintain relationships with people who aren't Christians, and protect the time that we spend with them. We can seek to follow Andrew's example. He could have stayed with Jesus for longer, and when he returned to his family he could have stayed quiet about his encounter. He did neither of these things.

Speaking personally, my wife and I find it really important to form relationships with people outside the church, partly because it is so easy for a minister simply to focus on church members. My wife develops her own network of friends through school. I'll go to the pub with someone whom I've met through playing sport, or go mountain biking with a fellow enthusiast from the local bike shop.

Remember, the 'first thing Andrew did' was to find his brother Simon and tell him about Jesus. Seizing this second opportunity needs to be our first priority after we have met with Jesus.

'Out of the world'

The third opportunity that Andrew took was not only to tell, but to bring: he brought Peter to Jesus (v. 42). A favourite story of Nicky Gumbel's is the story of Albert McMakin—the man who brought Billy Graham to faith.[28] Even though the name of Albert McMakin is not by any means widely known, he played a crucial role in Christian witness around the world through the latter half of the last century. A lot of people have heard of Billy Graham! And over the years, he has seen some three million Christian commitments, sparking a boom in evangelism all over the world.[29] We may never dare to believe that anything we do could have such wide-reaching consequences, but all we are called to do is bring people to Jesus, as Andrew brought Peter, and as Albert brought Billy. Archbishop William Temple described this as 'the single greatest service that one man can do to another'.[30] Every other opportunity that our culture offers is as nothing compared to this one.

At the same time, we need to understand the beliefs and assumptions that people have if our invitation is to bear fruit. Although we have already considered this to some extent in relation to doubt, it is worth reflecting on it briefly again, in relation to faith sharing. How we listen to people and how we invite them will be crucial to the success of our invitation. First and foremost, we need to have a relationship of trust with them that ensures we have the right to offer the invitation in the first place. To build this relationship, we will need to have listened and understood where they are coming from on a range of issues such as family, work, and any other topics that are significant in their lives. This is part of the discernment process in understanding their worldview. It is in spending time with someone and showing respect for their position on important issues that we gain their trust and friendship. That friendship and concern should lead us to want to pray that God will speak to them and bless them. When the right opportunity arises, we can 'be prepared to give an answer to everyone who asks (us) to give the reason for the hope that (we) have. But (we can) do this with gentleness and respect' (1 Peter 3:15).

It is important to take the opportunity to share our faith rather than trying to win arguments. Being good friends with a wonderful Hindu family, my wife, children and I spend many pleasant hours eating and drinking with them. Most of our conversation involves sharing news about our children and our work as well as other current concerns. If discussion naturally moves into the area of spiritual things, then the friendship that we have built up over seven years allows me to speak about the centrality of Jesus Christ in my life. Regardless of whether someone expresses a faith in a religion or not, it is through our words and deeds together that they will see Jesus Christ in our lives.

We also need to find creative and attractive ways to bring our friends into the presence of Jesus. If we simply invite them to come to church on a Sunday, they may well say no. If we invite them to a men's breakfast, a women's lunch, or a family outreach social, where there is a lively speaker with a clear message, as well as a pleasant atmosphere and good opportunities to build relationships, then our friends are more likely to say yes. Just as eggs will not hatch in a refrigerator, so we need to create warm, friendly and inviting atmospheres, which nurture people spiritually so that they start to take the first tentative steps of faith. Later, they may begin to consider the claims of Jesus through one-to-one conversations, small group discussions or by coming to church services.

As we have seen, Andrew took opportunities. He stayed with Jesus, he told others about Jesus and he brought others to Jesus. He models for us a way of life in which we too dare to seize opportunities that can have consequences far beyond anything we could dream.

The serial 'opportunist'

But Andrew didn't stop there. The Gospels tell us that he kept on grasping opportunities. It was Andrew who brought the young boy with five loaves and two fish to Jesus (John 6:8). He saw this act of generosity as significant enough to bring to his Master's attention, although his faith was not big enough to know what Jesus might do with such an offering. Even his words to Jesus, 'but how far will (the loaves and fish) go among so many?' (v. 9), were no barrier to God's power at work, though, and this should give us confidence. Jesus is ready and willing to use our efforts, however tentative, to demonstrate his glory.

In John 12, Andrew was one of the disciples who brought the Greeks to Jesus: 'Now there were some Greeks among those who went up to worship at the Feast. They came to Philip, who was from Bethsaida in Galilee, with a request. "Sir," they said, "we would like to see Jesus." Philip went to tell Andrew; Andrew and Philip in turn told Jesus' (John 12:20–22). Don Carson notes, 'The Greeks who request to see Jesus not only represent the "whole world", but they stand in contrast to the Pharisees who are exasperated by Jesus' growing influence.'[31] Through this act, Jesus was able to declare to the nations the gospel of life through death (see John 12:23–26).

What a privilege Andrew had, in providing ways for Jesus to teach and reach out to people, just through grasping the opportunities presented to him. His was a key ministry of both invitation and bridge-building.

Patron saint of younger brothers

As I mentioned earlier, Andrew can be seen something of a patron saint to younger brothers. He is an example to those of us who may find ourselves living in the shadow of a brother or sister, whether they are biological or spiritual relatives (such as friends who have acted in a supportive, brotherly or sisterly way). Andrew managed to have a marked impact on those around him, even if his brother Peter did constantly upstage him, and there are many Christians down the centuries for whom this has been true. Whether we spend our lives centre-stage or watching from the wings, we can use the unique gifts that God has given to us to bring about the extension of his kingdom.

One of the most famous Christian younger brothers of the last 300 years was named Charles. He was part of a large family, having seven sisters and two elder brothers, while nine other siblings had died during birth or in infancy. He was born into vicarage life as the son of Samuel and Susannah. He was brought up under a domestic regime that, to us, might seem very strict—being seen but not heard; referring to his siblings not simply by their Christian names, but as Brother John, or Sister Martha—yet, in its day, his experience would have been considered fairly liberal. Being from an educated background, he followed his brothers, Samuel and John, to Oxford University, via Westminster School.

Samuel was older than Charles by some 18 years, and would have seemed more like a distant relative. John, however, was still at Oxford when Charles arrived to begin his studies, as he had recently become a lecturer in Ancient Greek. John tried to exercise some positive influence over his younger brother. Charles, however, is said to have replied to some kindly advice on leading a religious life, 'Would you have me to be a saint all at once?'[32]

Perhaps in spite of himself, a spiritual transformation did come over Charles. He began attending church more frequently and receiving Holy Communion once a week—a practice considered somewhat over-zealous at that time. Having started to get to grips with his own spiritual life, he gathered a small group of fellow students around him to encourage them on their own journeys. This 'Holy Club' was not popular among Charles' fellow students. The uncle of one of Charles' group, shocked by his nephew's new-found zeal, threatened to throw him out of college, but contented himself with going to the college authorities to ask them to combat this fanaticism.

Charles' brother John quickly became involved in the 'Holy Club' too and took over the leadership. It was, in fact, something of a prototype for the small groups, or homegroups, that are an integral part of many local churches today. The activities and members of this little Oxford group were to exert a major influence upon the church around the world over the following centuries.

The two brothers were, of course, Charles and John Wesley. Social historians have described the Methodist movement as having had a profound impact upon the fabric of the United Kingdom. While other European countries were undergoing political revolution during the mid- to late 1800s, religious revival in the UK led to transformations of a different kind. Instead of disintergration of the social fabric of society, Methodist revivalism brought a certain stability to this rapidly industrializing nation.

The relationship between Charles and John Wesley was not always an easy one, and nearly half way through their ministry they parted company as co-evangelists. Nevertheless, Charles was able to use his gifts to the glory of God. From his earliest years, he had a love for poetry and music, and he turned this love towards the glory of God. The *Oxford Dictionary of the English Church* describes him as 'the most gifted and indefatigable hymn writer that England has ever known'.[33] He wrote over 5500 hymns and used them to encourage worship, mission, prayer, devotion to God and instruction in Christian living. Even the most up-to-date hymn books today, which may otherwise emphasize contemporary worship songs, still include many of Wesley's hymns, such as 'Hark! the herald angels sing', 'Love divine, all loves excelling' and 'And can it be?'

Charles Wesley was a preacher and a pastor, but he is best remembered as a hymn writer. Like Andrew, he was a younger brother who saw his sibling step into the limelight and draw others around him; yet, like Andrew, he played his part in transforming people's lives by leading them to Christ, using his gifts and seizing opportunities as they came.

Use us as we are

One of the joys of having a hobby that you are passionate about is that—unless yours is a very obscure pastime—you can read all about it. There are four mountain bike magazines on the market that I will occasionally purchase. Then I can focus my energies upon contemplating the next upgrade for my bike, planning a long-distance journey for the forthcoming year, even learning some new riding techniques. And I can do this all from the comfort of my armchair! It is ironic that active outdoor hobbies can be maintained in this way. We like to think that we are maintaining a healthy lifestyle as we live such sedentary lives, but all the time we are fooling ourselves by putting off the opportunity for activity until tomorrow. Or the next day…!

As we think about our own situations, we might think of opportunities we have missed. We may feel a bit like the person who, in the words of James, 'listens to the word but does not do what it says'. According to James, this person 'is like a man who looks at his face in a mirror and, after looking at himself, goes away and immediately forgets what he looks like' (James 1:23–24). We miss the opportunity when we don't listen to the word that gives life, but just as we can change our mind and choose physical exercise, so we can listen to God's call and grasp the opportunity for life-enhancing spiritual activity in the service of Jesus Christ.

Alternatively, we might find that we empathize most closely with Andrew out of all the disciples, because he sounds something like us. God has created us to be one of his 'opportunists' as well. We may not find it easy to argue for the claims of Christianity. We may not enjoy standing centre-stage, like a John Wesley, a Billy Graham or a Simon Peter, but we may get a deep sense of satisfaction when other people seek God as we pray for and encourage them. What-ever our personality, each of us has different gifts, a different calling in life and different ways of hearing and responding to God's call, yet each of us also can have the privilege and opportunity of saying with Andrew the most life-changing words of all: 'We have found the Messiah.'

Questions for reflection

1. Imagine Jesus turning around to you and saying, 'What do you want?' What would your answer be?
2. Do you set aside time to 'be with' Jesus? Consider whether this is quality time or hurried time.
3. If you are like Andrew and do not like to take centre-stage, what can you do to introduce others to Jesus?

Matthew at a fork in the road

After this, Jesus went out and saw a tax collector by the name of Levi sitting at his tax booth. 'Follow me,' Jesus said to him, and Levi got up, left everything and followed him. Then Levi held a great banquet for Jesus at his house, and a large crowd of tax collectors and others were eating with them. But the Pharisees and the teachers of the law who belonged to their sect complained to his disciples, 'Why do you eat and drink with tax collectors and "sinners"?' Jesus answered them, 'It is not the healthy who need a doctor, but the sick. I have not come to call the righteous, but sinners to repentance.'

LUKE 5:27–32

Imagine that you are on a journey. You are travelling alone, although in times past you have travelled with others on the road. Separated from any companions, you come to an intersection on the path. One way is steep, narrow and winding; the other looks easier, devoid of apparent difficulty. When the path was a single track, you did not face the chance to get it right or wrong, but you do now. Still, you must choose. As we consider the disciple called Matthew, or Levi, we see that he had to make a profound decision: whether to continue his life along the same road or take a different way.

Many years ago, there was a man called Eric Liddell, who was a theological student at Edinburgh University, preparing for church ministry. He was also an athlete, a fast runner. He decided to discontinue his theological studies in order to train for the Olympics properly. After a number of qualifying events, he reached the 1924 Paris Olympic Games as a member of the British team.

Once there, however, he decided to drop out of the 100-yards sprint because the event was scheduled to take place on a Sunday, and in his eyes that would involve 'breaking the sabbath'. Coaches, politicians, team-mates, even British royalty, tried to persuade him to run, but he would not budge. It was a matter of conscience. He had decided. On the suggestion of his team-mate, Harold Abrahams, he swapped events and competed in the 400-yard dash, winning the gold medal and setting a world record that stood for more than a decade.

Sir Winston Churchill is considered by many to have been the greatest Prime Minister that Britain has ever had. In hindsight, it is easy to see his steadfastness as simply 'the right thing to do', but the history of the early years of World War II tells a different story. With the fall of France, Britain stood alone against the invading Nazi forces. It would have been easy to sue for peace, or to surrender in the face of terror.

This was Churchill's response when he spoke to the House of Commons: 'I have nothing to offer but blood, toil, tears, and sweat. We have before us an ordeal of the most grievous kind. We have before us many, many months of struggle and suffering.'[34] In the light of the facts, he could offer only one option to the British people: war by land, sea and air. He could allow for only one outcome: victory. Any other outcome would be catastrophic.

My final story is of a British businessman named John Laing, a name that is familiar to millions because of the sign above construction sites across the United Kingdom. At the age of 30, his building business was in severe financial difficulty, but he made a commitment that he later summed up in these words: 'First, the centre of my life was to be God—God as seen in Jesus Christ. Secondly, I was going to enjoy life and help others to enjoy it.' To this end, in 1909, he drew up a financial plan to determine his present and future giving. 'If my income is £1,000 per year, I will give away £200, live on £300, save £500.' Yet Sir John went beyond this principle. When his will was published after his death, many people were amazed at the size of the estate: just £371. As his biographer commented, 'The man who had handled millions had given them all away.'[35]

What holds these three stories together is the power of decision, the God-given ability that each of us has to decide in all manner of situations.[36]

No one understood this better than Jesus Christ. He knew the power with which humankind had been endued in their decision-making ability. Jesus made invitations to people all the time. He called them to respond, to decide to follow him. He could have commanded people to action: after all, he commanded the winds and the waves to obey him (Matthew 8:26). But he didn't. Yes, he spoke authoritatively, but Jesus always allowed for the possibility that his invitations would be rejected. Human beings, unlike the winds and the waves, have been given free will to turn away from God's rule. We can see several examples in the Gospels: '"Lord, if it's you," Peter replied, "tell me to come to you on the water." "Come," (Jesus) said' (Matthew 14:28–29). 'Then (Jesus) said to the man, "Stretch out your hand." So he stretched it out and it was completely restored, just as sound as the other' (Matthew 12:13). 'Jesus straightened up and asked her, "Woman, where are they? Has no one condemned you?" "No one, sir," she said. "Then neither do I condemn you," Jesus declared. "Go now and leave your life of sin"' (John 8:10–11).

All of these encounters demonstrate the way that Jesus called people to make radical decisions that transform lives. None of them is based upon easy choices. All of them have a high element of risk and trust required of the respondent. Nevertheless, each time a response is made, a life is turned around. It is worth remembering that some people chose to reject the inviation to follow Jesus. The rich young ruler exercised his free will by walking away: 'When the young man heard this, he went away sad, because he had great wealth' (Matthew 19:22). Jesus invites; we respond.

As someone who does a lot of public speaking, I know that you can tell a lot about the effect of your words by the listeners' response afterwards. 'That was interesting' can mean that while I may have tickled the brain's thought-capacity, I probably haven't achieved much else. 'That was a nice talk' can mean I was so unchallenging that the listener unconsciously felt that my words were designed to help them sit more comfortably! Sometimes, somebody may be angry. This either means that I have successfully challenged them, or that I have been so unclear as to offend them unintentionally. From the evidence of the Gospels, few people ever walked away from Jesus thinking that his talks were simply 'nice' or 'interesting'. His words called for lifestyle choice. People would not have forgotten his teaching after Sunday lunch.

'You're a what?'

As we explore what it means to be a disciple today, and as we think about what can inhibit us from following Jesus Christ, the calling of Levi has profound significance. The name Levi in Hebrew means 'pledged for a debt', which is quite appropriate because he was a tax collector. It may be that he had two names (Jewish people in Jesus' day often did). There may be a story behind Luke's choice of this name. It does, in fact, sum up the tax collector's life situation, as Levi is indeed 'pledged'. His life is committed to the way that he has chosen: tax collecting.

On our journey of faith, we may have a name by which we are known. Sometimes other people may have a word in their minds that they automatically use to describe us. We may be 'angry' or 'submissive'. Like one of the companions of Christian, in Bunyan's *Pilgrim's Progress*, we might be 'timid'. Conversely, we might give ourselves a name that sums up our character. It might be 'scared' or 'competitive'. That name, like Levi's, may seem incompatible with the Christian faith, or incompatible with the steps of discipleship that we want to make. We too may be 'pledged' to something or someone that keeps us apart from God. Just as Levi had to consider what he was pledged to, so we must consider our 'name'. If we are 'competitive', are we pledged to winning? If we are 'timid', are we pledged to submission? Once we have come to a greater sense of self-awareness, then we will be able to consider how we should respond.

In the New Testament era, tax collectors were notorious for swindling people. When the Romans conquered Israel, they appropriated a long-standing system of tolls and duties collected at ports, major road junctions and city gates. Levi would have collected tax on about two to five per cent of the value of the goods being transported through these places, and if goods were on a long journey, they could be subject to multiple taxation.

To get the job, a tax collector would have to go to the authorities and bid for a town or area where he could collect taxes. Whoever put up the highest bid would 'win' the area. So, if you wanted to be the tax collector for Galilee, you might bid the equivalent of £10,000,000. If you won the contract, you would be pledged to deliver that amount to the Romans. Any money you raised over and above this amount, you could keep for yourself. As a result, this process led to rampant extortion. Only by charging more than was due could tax collectors make significant profits, and there was no regulation as to how much they could charge: it was usually as much as they thought they could get away with.

This made tax collectors very unpopular with the local people, even more so because they were seen as collaborators with the occupying power. Moreover, they were considered ritually unclean on account of their continual contact with Gentiles, and were banned from the synagogue because of their need to work on the sabbath. (Although devout Jews would not move goods around on the sabbath, Gentile traders and travellers would. They would therefore be liable to taxation, so the tax collector had to be ready seven days a week to make his profit.) The tax collectors' job is commonly linked with that of prostitutes in the New Testament, and with 'robbers' by the rabbis. Honest tax collectors were so rare that the historian Josephus tells how a town was so impressed with the service of its honest tax collector that it erected a statue in his honour! Even knowing all of this, it is difficult to place ourselves in the New Testament world and imagine quite how much tax collectors were hated. The closest parallel may be to the way people today react to the presence of child abusers in their community.

To cap it all, Levi was not even a particularly successful tax collector. He was one of the hired hands sitting in the tax booth, not one of the bosses behind the scenes. How he ended up as a tax collector, we don't know. Perhaps, like most of us, he didn't think about the wrong choice he was making until after it had happened. Very often, we do not know why we make our choices. They just seem to happen, without very much thought on our part. Levi may not have positively chosen the life of a tax collector—the abuse, isolation, hatred and perhaps even self-loathing that went with it. Equally, politicians don't begin a career in public service with one eye on corruption. Christian ministers don't begin their vocation with the intention of exercising spiritual power over people in an abusive way. Treasurers of charitable organizations don't usually take on the job with the aim of embezzling funds. They may just drift into wrongdoing.

We human beings do have a tendency to drift into error, while we have to make a positive decision for what is right. I once spent some time with offenders in Camp Hill Prison on the Isle of Wight, where I learnt at first hand that the primary reason why those released from prison often reoffend is the lack of a positive alternative to a life of crime. Without an alternative friendship network to help people reintegrate into society, ex-offenders can feel that their options are very limited. Even in prison, inmates who had made a Christian commitment found it very difficult to maintain a Christian lifestyle there, even though they could rely upon the support of an understanding chaplaincy team. Equally, no one just drifts into a life of prayer, Christian fellowship and an intimate relationship with God. They have to decide to do so.

Dallas Willard makes the point that ever since the Protestant Reformation, there has been an emphasis upon 'salvation through faith alone'. This is a good and true doctrine but, he argues, it distracts people from considering the importance of 'working out our salvation' (Philippians 2:12). To pick up the analogy from the beginning of the chapter, instead of standing at the fork in the road and consciously choosing the 'steep and rugged pathway', we expect God to accept that we *meant* to choose the rugged way even if we actually chose the easier path.

There is a widespread notion that just passing through death transforms human character. Discipleship is not needed. Just believe enough to 'make it'. But I have never been able to find any basis in scriptural tradition or psychological reality to think that this might be so. What if death only forever fixes us as the kind of person we are at death? What would we do in heaven with a debauched character and a hate-filled heart? Surely something must be done now. And that brings us back to the matter of intention and decision.[37]

Indecision time

Discipleship and decision are inseparable. Each one of us has to decide to take up new ways of living for Christ, or lay down destructive behaviours. The psychological reality of the cost of discipleship—and the hard decisions involved—is demonstrated in the story of the rich young man, found in Matthew 19:16–22.

'Now a man came up to Jesus and asked, "Teacher, what good thing must I do to get eternal life?"' (v. 16). The rich young man (or 'rich young ruler' as he is sometimes called) comes to Jesus to ask what Dietrich Bonhoeffer calls the 'ultimate, serious question in the whole world'.[38] In trying to ask this question, however, his true intention is revealed as he actually asks another: 'What good thing must I do?' (sometimes translated from the Greek, 'Good Teacher, what must I do?'). On the basis of either translation, the young man is making eternal life into an academic exercise, which he will discuss with a good teacher, in order to receive some good advice. Jesus, however, is interested in helping him to respond to God, not dilly-dallying around with late-night-coffee conversation, so he points him back to God and his commandments.

The rich young man's evasion and inaction are demonstrated further by his answer to Jesus' reminder to 'obey the commandments' (v. 17b). The young man proceeds to ask questions of Jesus to distract him from the real issue—what he should do with his life.

It is often by the continual raising of problems that we try to wriggle out of responsibilities. Dietrich Bonhoeffer reminds us, 'The Serpent in Paradise put [those disobedient thoughts] into the mind of the first man by asking, "Hath God said?" ... Only the Devil has an answer for our moral difficulties, and he says: "Keep on posing problems, and you will escape the necessity of obedience."'[39] With the rich young man, Jesus cuts through all his questions with a challenge, expressed in love: 'If you want to be perfect, go, sell your possessions and give to the poor, and you will have treasure in heaven. Then come, follow me' (v. 21). Voluntary poverty was the means; discipleship was the end: 'Follow me.' The Gospel account goes on to tell us that the rich young ruler 'went away sad, because he had great wealth' (v. 22). We can assume from the passage that the indecision in his heart led to an answer, and the answer was 'no'.

We often come to Jesus with questions—questions about suffering, family relationships, lifestyle choices, and many more. Like the rich young ruler, we may come in faith, seeing Jesus as a good teacher, yet he still cuts through our questions by asking us one of his own: 'Will you follow me?' We can keep on asking, or we can listen, and then answer. Our questions, legitimate as they may be, can sometimes wait. That was the difference between the rich young ruler and Levi. Levi understood when the questions should stop and the response should be made; the rich young ruler did not. He wanted theological debate when he was being called to action.

It's not God in the box

Maybe Levi had heard Jesus on other occasions. Jesus' relationships with outsiders and so-called 'low-lifes' were renowned. Perhaps he had preached in that area before. Perhaps Levi had stood on the edge of one of those crowds or overheard Jesus converse with another 'sinner' as he passed by his tax-collecting booth.

Maybe we have heard the gospel message on a number of occasions. We know what Jesus is all about—his sacrifice on the cross for our sin, his death so that we can have life, his resurrection to demonstrate the new life that we can have in him. More information was not what Levi needed; more information may not be what we need. Levi needed to respond. This was his crisis moment. We too have turning-point moments when God provides us with the chance to step out and journey into a future that may seem dangerous and uncertain, although it is actually a secure future in the presence of God.

So Jesus spoke one of the shortest sentences of invitation in human speech. We can picture Levi standing in his tax booth—in his box, if you like. Levi had become stuck in his box and the life he had probably drifted into—the sins of thought, word or deed that he habitually fell into, the life choices he didn't aspire to when he was young but which had just happened over the years. We may feel stuck with the 'names' and attitudes that we have drifted into. We may feel timid when we wish we were assertive, or angry when we wish we were calm. However impossible it might seem to change, Jesus breaks through and says to Levi and to us, 'Follow me.'

To put something 'in a box' implies that we have contained it. We 'pigeonhole' people by their job description or their marital status. When we have contained something or someone in a box, we can control it—even shut the lid on it. The phrase 'God in a box' has come to represent the way we try to limit God's freedom. It has always been part of human nature to seek to control God, whether in the Judeo-Christian tradition or in other faith forms. We may feel that other religions or Christian denominations constrict and constrain God but that we ourselves don't do it. We might not use grand rituals to signify the understanding of God's character, but still we find other ways to make false boundaries. Perhaps it is through the narrowness of our biblical interpretations, filtering the meaning of Jesus' words through our favourite church tradition. Perhaps we restrict God to only a small portion of our lives—say, an hour and a half on Sundays. Or perhaps we believe that our own will for our life is really God's will, and we use his name as some kind of spiritual endorsement for our own choices.

Levi was the one in the box, not God. We might think that we are allowing God to be sovereign when in fact we are limiting his movement in our lives. God will not be constrained, and Jesus has an exit strategy that includes Levi, as well as us, if we will respond.

The cost of discipleship

We should not deceive ourselves that following Jesus means an easy life. Yes, we can know joy and peace in meeting with Christ and walking in his steps, but there inevitably comes a time when the way grows more difficult. One of the most inspiring Christian disciples of the 20th century was a man I have already mentioned, who had to make a series of tough decisions for Christ. Dietrich Bonhoeffer was born in 1906 in Breslau, Germany (now Wroclaw, Poland), the sixth child of a well-to-do family with a strong Christian background. His childhood years were dominated by World War I, during which his older brothers, Karl-Friedrich and Walter, enlisted. Karl-Friedrich was severely injured, while Walter died after a painful operation to remove shrapnel. The twelve-year-old Dietrich and his whole family were deeply affected by the loss.

These wartime experiences played a part in Dietrich's decision to become a pastor and theologian. At that time, a crisis was developing in the German church. Pastors and theologians were separating into two camps—those who were drawn to international dialogue with other Christians, and those who supported the German National Church and National Socialism. (National Socialism—or Nazism, as it is better known—was the political ideology developed by Adolf Hitler. The German National Church gave credence to the racist and supremacist views of the ideology through developing a supportive theology.)

Ordained in 1931, Bonhoeffer's sermons and speeches were powerful and sometimes prophetic. In 1932, a year before Hitler came to power, he preached at the Kaiser Wilhelm Memorial Church, Berlin, saying:

We should not be surprised if the time comes for the church too, when the blood of the martyrs will be called for. But this blood, if we really have the courage to shed it, will not be so innocent and shining as that of the first witnesses. On our blood will lie our great guilt: the guilt of the useless servant.

He did not temper his views even when Hitler took control of the country. On the one and only occasion that he was asked to broadcast with the Berlin Broadcasting Company, he was asked to consider the concept of leadership. His broadcast included the following words.

If a leader allows himself to be persuaded by those he leads who want to turn him into an idol—and those who are led will always hope for this— then the image of the leader will degenerate into that of the 'misleader'. The leader who makes an idol of himself and his office makes a mockery of God.[40]

Life-and-death choices

Bonhoeffer was offered a pastorate in a German-speaking church in London, and wrote to his friend and mentor, Karl Barth, asking his advice. Barth's reply was forthright: 'You ought to drop all these intellectual frills and special pleadings, however interesting, and concentrate on one thing alone, that you are a German and that your Church's house is on fire, that you know enough and also know how to say it well enough, to be capable of bringing help.'[41] This was his eventual course of action, and he emerged as the leader of the Confessing Church (so called because it remained free from Nazi influence). Bonhoeffer's theologically rooted opposition to the Nazi regime made him a natural first leader (along with Barth, among others). This church resisted anti-semitism and Aryan superiority, and Bonhoeffer, based at a theological seminary for the Confessing Church until its enforced closure by the Nazis, wrote and taught that state injustice and oppression were not to be tolerated.

During the late 1930s, Bonhoeffer had the opportunity to travel, visiting London and New York, where he spent time studying at the Union Theological Seminary. On returning to Germany in 1939, he started working with key figures in German military espionage, who were secretly trying to undermine the Nazi war effort. All the while, he continued his theological work for the German Confessing Church. The security organization that he worked for (the *Abwehr*) came into increasing conflict with the Gestapo, who had grown suspicious of its activities, until, on 5 April 1943, Bonhoeffer was arrested. He was imprisoned in Tegel Military Prison, Berlin, and was held there for 18 months with a number of his fellow conspirators. He wrote many letters and notes from prison, which demonstrate his resolute and sometimes even optimistic mood.[42] The approach of the Allied invasion force meant that he was eventually moved to Buchenwald concentration camp. The day before his execution, he held a service for his fellow prisoners, and on 9 April 1945 he was hanged along with his friends and co-conspirators. Twenty-one days later, Adolf Hitler committed suicide, and the war came to an end shortly thereafter

In his poem, 'Stations on the Road to Freedom', written in prison, Bonhoeffer sums up his view of discipleship:

> *Faint not nor fear, but go out in to the storms of action,*
> *Trusting God whose commandment you faithfully follow;*
> *Freedom, exultant, will welcome your spirit with joy.*[43]

The cost of non-discipleship

As awe-inspiring and humbling as the story of Bonhoeffer is, his commitment and sacrifice should not cause us to lose heart. It is tempting for us think, 'If I was asked to stand up for Jesus, even to death, I know I would deny him.' Bonhoeffer's story demonstrates the 'cost of discipleship' (and that is the title of one of his best-known books), but there is also a 'cost of non-discipleship', as Richard Foster points out:

The cost of non-discipleship is far greater—even when this life alone is considered—than the price to walk with Jesus. Non-discipleship costs abiding peace, a life penetrated throughout by love, faith that sees everything in the light of God's overriding governance for good, hopefulness that stands firm in the most discouraging of circumstances, power to do what is right and withstand the forces of evil. In short, it costs exactly that abundance of life Jesus said he came to bring (John 10:10).[44]

We may back away from Jesus' call, but there is also a cost. Equally, we should not lose heart when we reflect upon the huge sacrifice of a man like Dietrich Bonhoeffer or we will despair altogether. If we choose to follow Jesus, we can be assured that God will give us the strength to follow him if we ask.

Gift of God

We can be tempted to take great pains over little decisions, avoiding larger ones because they seem out of reach. For Levi, the big decision was not out of reach. He got up and followed Jesus, leaving everything. Such a decision simply requires us to take the first step, then another, and another. A big decision is often made up of lots of little decisions. Jesus' teaching in the Sermon on the Mount (Matthew 5—7) reminds us that if we prioritize God and his kingdom in the big decisions of life, all other decisions can be set within a kingdom focus (see Matthew 6:33).

Jesus gave Levi a new name: Matthew, meaning 'gift of God'. No longer was he Levi: 'pledged for a debt'. Now that his name means 'gift of God', and because God has given him the gift of freedom, Matthew shares it with others and throws a party. Matthew is now the talk of his outcast community. He's the one who has left his job, his money and his place in the pecking order, and he will never go back. He will use his writing skills to craft a Gospel. He will invite people into the presence of Jesus, so that they can decide about him for themselves.

Like Matthew, we may find ourselves in a place in our lives that we have just drifted into. Like Matthew, we may be in a box that we don't really like, but that we've grown used to. We might even have a nickname or label that sounds as if we have to pay a debt of some kind. Whatever our circumstances, we can follow Levi's example and respond to Jesus. We can turn our back on that unwanted part of our lives, walk away from the sin we have drifted into, and recognize that Jesus, the good physician, can heal our pain and forgive our sin. We can tell our friends that we're making a new start. It's decision time, and Jesus says to us, 'Follow me.'

Questions for reflection

1. As you reflect upon your Christian life over the last twelve months, is it marked by drift or decision?
2. Are there ways in which you put God in a box to limit his power on your life?
3. When you reflect upon Bonhoeffer's determination to take a stand, does it strengthen you or make you feel anxious? Why?

4

James on the downhill slope

Then James and John, the sons of Zebedee, came to him. 'Teacher,' they said, 'we want you to do for us whatever we ask.' 'What do you want me to do for you?' he asked. They replied, 'Let one of us sit at your right and the other at your left in your glory.' 'You don't know what you are asking,' Jesus said. 'Can you drink the cup I drink or be baptized with the baptism I am baptized with?' 'We can,' they answered. Jesus said to them, 'You will drink the cup I drink and be baptized with the baptism I am baptized with, but to sit at my right or left is not for me to grant. These places belong to those for whom they have been prepared.' When the ten heard about this, they became indignant with James and John. Jesus called them together and said, 'You know that those who are regarded as rulers of the Gentiles lord it over them, and their high officials exercise authority over them. Not so with you. Instead, whoever wants to become great among you must be your servant, and whoever wants to be first must be slave of all. For even the Son of Man did not come to be served, but to serve, and to give his life as a ransom for many.'

MARK 10:35–45

As we come to the character of James, I want to consider the human trait of selfishness. In the Bible reading above, you will have noticed that the story relates to a request by both James and John to Jesus. There are a number of reasons why it might be helpful to focus upon just one of the brothers. Firstly, we need to own up to selfishness. It is very easy to blame someone else for our behaviour. If you have brothers or sisters, you may remember from your childhood saying, 'He (or she) made me do it!' By focusing on one of the disciples in this story, I want to avoid the chance of James somehow pinning the blame on his brother! The second reason for looking at James is that he plays a lesser role than his brother John in the Gospel stories, and it is interesting to try to get into the mind of one of the disciples about whom we know relatively little. The third reason is that John seems to be an incredibly complex character in the Gospels. Is the brother of James the same John who wrote the fourth Gospel? Is one of the 'sons of thunder' (Mark 3:17) also the 'beloved disciple' (John 19:26)? The scope of this chapter doesn't allow me to go into the deep theological issues that this matter raises, although there is a great deal of writing that makes this debate accessible to the interested reader.[45] For these three reasons, we shall consider James alone, rather than both James and John.

On a downhill slope

There is something exhilarating about riding downhill fast: ask any skier or cyclist! Gravity is one of God's wonderful inventions—especially when it helps you to experience speed and an adrenalin rush. Part of the thrill of downhill mountain biking comes from the unpredictability of the slope. As you rush headlong, using all your concentration to help you steer the bike and manoeuvre your body so that you are correctly balanced and anticipate oncoming obstacles, it feels good to be alive. One of the primary devices that helps to keep you alive after taking a calculated risk on a descent is a good pair of brakes. When I built a bike from scratch in a workshop, the one area where I took particular care was with the alignment of the disk brakes to the brake pads. Brakes that don't work or have been poorly serviced are as lethal on a bike as they are in a car.

James is on a downhill slope, but of a different kind. Like many of us, he is inclined towards selfishness. He begins a conversation with Jesus that he is unable to stop. There are many hidden dangers in the words he chooses, and he does not see them. He does not seem to have the ability to stop the conversation and put on the brakes. Once he has made the initial comment, the gravity of selfishness keeps pulling him down to the bottom. As we consider the situation, we can learn from his mistakes and reflect on how we might overcome the temptation to behave in similar ways ourselves.

The road you're on

James was one of the disciples who were part of Jesus' inner circle. Not only was he part of the Twelve, but he was also one of Jesus' closest followers. He was privileged to be present at the raising of Jairus' daughter (Luke 8:51). He was on the mountain at the transfiguration of Jesus (Mark 9:2). Later, he was to be there during the agony of Jesus in the garden of Gethsemene. James had left his fishing nets (Mark 1:19) and his part in what must have been a substantial family business, and he had been on a rollercoaster ride of discipleship ever since. I'm sure that if you had asked him, James would have echoed the words of his fellow fisherman, Peter: 'To whom shall we go but Jesus? He has the words of eternal life' (John 6:68). Yes, James was committed to journeying with Jesus—all the way to Jerusalem.

Both Mark and Luke describe the encounter between James and Jesus on the road to Jerusalem. It shows how James, for all his experience of Jesus' ministry, reveals his true colours when Jesus' mind is made up. Jesus is determined to go up to Jerusalem to fulfil his mission from God. Jesus is on the move. What about James? In which direction does he want to go?

James had heard Jesus teach that he was going to Jerusalem to bring in the messianic age. He assumed that this meant a 'heavenly banquet' for all God-fearing Jews, and he (with his brother) wanted to be the first in line. They assumed that the banquet would soon be served and so they were vying for places at the top table. With his brother John, James said to Jesus, 'We want you to do for us whatever we ask… Let one of us sit at your right and the other at your left in your glory' (Mark 10:35, 37).

Heaven is sometimes portrayed in the Bible as a celebratory meal. It is likened to a victory banquet where the hero of the battle—the Messiah in this case—is honoured. In the book of the prophet Isaiah, the writer says, 'On this mountain the Lord Almighty will prepare a feast of rich food for all peoples, a banquet of aged wine— the best of meats and the finest of wines' (Isaiah 25:6). We read in Psalm 23:5a, 'You prepare a table before me in the presence of my enemies.' In the New Testament, Jesus frequently uses the image of the banquet to describe heaven: 'The kingdom of heaven is like a king who prepared a wedding banquet for his son' (Matthew 22:2). Later in the same Gospel, he tells the parable of the ten virgins (Matthew 25:1–13). Here, the five 'wise virgins' are those who are ready with plenty of oil in their lamps to welcome the bridegroom to the wedding banquet as it grows dark. The foolish virgins are those who have no spare fuel for their lamps and so are not prepared to play their part in the celebrations. This imagery of the banquet points to Jesus as the bridegroom, and the message of the parable is made clear in verse 13: 'Therefore keep watch, because you do not know the day or the hour.'

Accordingly, we can understand James and John wanting to ask their question of Jesus. If Jesus is to be the focus of the banquet— as the son (in Matthew 22) or the bridegroom (in Matthew 25)— then he is the one to approach. If the disciples are exhorted to keep watch (Matthew 25:13), then it seems entirely appropriate to ask their question as soon as possible. James and his brother did not really know what they were asking for, nor did they realize how insensitive their ambition and selfishness were in the light of what Jesus was about to do. They were looking for a crown without a cross, honour without humility, and glory without suffering.

Let's look at the words of James in more detail, because they reveal his attitude of heart and perhaps also our own.

'We want'

'Want' is a word that everyone learns very early in their lives. You don't need to define it with the accuracy of a dictionary ('to feel a need or a longing for'[46]) to know how to use it. Children start to use the word as soon as they can speak. It is the word we first jump to when we feel that we are lacking something. Moreover, our consumer culture bombards us with attractions that appeal to all our senses, stimulating us to 'want' ever more. Ironically, in the last few minutes, while I have been writing, I have just received delivery of a frame and wheels so that I can build myself a new mountain bike! I justify this to myself because the bike building gives me a challenging hobby, and the exercise that I take—when I've built the bike—keeps me refreshed. Of course, not all 'wanting' is bad. Some of it is essential to life. We want sleep, food, shelter and many other necessities. Added to that, the Bible says that God longs to give us good gifts: as the psalmist says, 'He satisfies the thirsty and fills the hungry with good things' (Psalm 107:9).

James' question is not the question of a child who points and blurts out the word 'want', however. It is the question of a mature person who has considered the moment and chosen the time to ask. His question is a very open-ended one—so open-ended that it is not really a question so much as a statement: 'We want you to do whatever we ask.'

We too tend to ask Jesus to do whatever we want him to. There are two kinds of requests that we might make. We might ask Jesus to provide us with an expensive car, simply for our pleasure and enjoyment. A more subtle and complex request, however, might be that we should receive more power and authority within the church, or greater status within our peer group. We ask because we think that by receiving whatever it is we want, we shall become happy and fulfilled. But we can then justify the request by saying that it would be for the 'good of God's kingdom': it will enable us to serve God more effectively. The quest for personal fulfilment is not limited to our daily needs, but also to our view of discipleship, just like James.

This failure to see the motivation behind the question is repeated today in churches and Christian communities throughout the land. It is not just that we say to Jesus, 'We want...'. It is not even that we verbally articulate that we want Jesus to do 'whatever we ask'. It is that our underlying attitude demonstrates the condition of our heart.

Pure intention

Here we come to the heart of the matter, the question that always seems so hard to answer truthfully: what is our real motive for asking Jesus for something? In prayer, we spend significant amounts of time making requests of God. We ask for all kinds of things, for all kinds of reasons—some wholesome, some selfish, most with mixed motives. Glimpsing what God was doing with Jesus, James seems to have acted from the natural impulse to turn the situation to his own advantage. 'Jesus is going to Jerusalem,' he thinks. 'There must be a messianic banquet coming soon. I'll go along as well, with the hope of getting a seat at the top table.' Such naked ambition, however, is not part of the value system of God's kingdom.

As I mentioned earlier, Jesus told a parable of a king who prepared a wedding banquet for his son (Matthew 22:2–14). The first guests to be invited refuse to come to the banquet, and abuse and even kill the messengers who bring them the invitation. Next, the king invites others, who do choose to attend the wedding banquet. Some of them, however, do not come dressed in their wedding clothes. One man is challenged by the king about his choice of clothes and is speechless, his silence demonstrating his guilt. The parable suggests that his guilt is in coming to the banquet on his own terms—disregarding the need for appropriate attire. Another piece of teaching by Jesus, found in Matthew, Mark, and Luke, is a warning that his disciples should beware of teachers who go around in flowing robes 'and have the most important seats in the synagogues and the places of honour at banquets' (Mark 12:39). As this comes shortly after James and John's request to Jesus, they must have felt very self-conscious about their earlier question.

Jesus' attitude towards status and rank goes against the values of the secular world. He spells it out in his response to James and John: 'Not so with you. Instead, whoever wants to become great among you must be your servant, and whoever wants to be first must be slave of all. For even the Son of Man did not come to be served, but to serve, and to give his life as a ransom for many' (Mark 10:44–45). James had also heard Jesus say, 'If anyone would come after me, he must deny himself and take up his cross and follow me' (Mark 8:34). James wanted the rewards of the kingdom before he truly understood the relationship with the king, and quite often, so do we.

If James' heart is characterized by selfishness, Jesus' heart is characterized by love. Notice the loving, patient way that he responds to James and John: he allows them to ask their question (v. 36). This is a relief to me. It tells me that however foolish and self-centred my prayers are, however much I have forgotten the way of the cross, I can still bring my egotistical requests to Christ, and his love for me is such that he will not reject me. Jesus seeks to maintain relationship with us, his selfish disciples, by hearing our sometimes ludicrous requests. He demonstrates long-suffering mercy so that we can continue to learn that it is only through being with him that we find true happiness—not through the material rewards we hope to gain.

'Let one of us sit at your right and the other at your left'

It is no great surprise that the two brothers asked this question together. James and John had probably talked at great length about how they might broach the issue, when the right time would be. It is such an audacious request that they probably needed each other to help them muster the courage. And the heart of their request shows what lies in their hearts: greed—greed for status, greed for power and, in the context of the banqueting metaphor, greed for food!

Matthew's Gospel tells of a similar request to Jesus, located at a similar stage in the story (Matthew 20:18–28). Jesus has explained that he must suffer and die, and he has set his face towards Jerusalem. He knows that this will lead to a confrontation with the chief priests and his eventual crucifixion. This time, however, it is the mother of James and John who asks if they may sit at the Lord's left and right hand. Could it be that Matthew's Gospel, supposedly written later than Mark's, was trying to conceal the selfish attitude of Christian saints who had become pillars of the church?[47] Or is it that the self-promoting tendency had been inherited by 'her boys' from a pushy mother? Perhaps there were two separate incidents that the Gospel writers chose to locate at this point in order to contrast the attitude of Jesus with those around him. Whatever the answer, greed and self-promotion seem to have been something of a family trait in the Zebedee family.

In the film *Wall Street* (1987), Michael Douglas, playing the part of Gordon Gekko, a high-flying financier, makes a fulsome justification for the merits of greed: 'The point is that greed, for lack of a better word, is good. Greed is right. Greed works. Greed clarifies, cuts through and captures the essence of the evolutionary spirit.'[48] Some Christians have also sought to justify the human desire for profit or fame or just plain self-betterment by arguing that it is behind most of society's advances. Self-interest will lead a drug company to come up with a product that they will sell for profit, but that product might also be a miracle cure. Others might argue that ambition is a God-given trait, but that when it is taken to excess it becomes greed. We need to recognize our responsibility to care for one another as well as to see our ambitions fulfilled. Many Christians have a great capacity to work in entrepreneurial ways, which, in turn, can lead to the creation of jobs and a benefit to society. (Remember the story of John Laing in chapter 3.)

Nevertheless, it is too easy to find ourselves seeking theological justification for our consumer-driven culture. This culture builds in dissatisfaction with the products that we buy, so that manufacturers can persuade us to replace what we have for something new. There is nothing intrinsically wrong with enjoying the purchase of products that we have carefully chosen and diligently saved up for, which enhance our lives in some way. Greed, however, is often the most powerful force at work in our lives, and we need to apply a Christian mind to our lifestyle choices so that we choose generosity instead of greed.

John Wesley, the founder of Methodism, was a wonderful example of somebody who resisted greed and practised generosity. Sales of his writings earned him £1400 annually (an enormous sum of money in his day), but he kept only £30 for himself. For a man of such standing, he wore simple clothes and ate inexpensive food. We do not need a calling to voluntary poverty to live generously and still enjoy good things. To have attractive clothes at a price we can afford, we simply have to wait for the sales to come round. In a time when so many people are buying new clothes, charity shops are often filled with cast-off designer labels.

Care with our finances should never be an end in itself, though. Rather, it should release us to carry out acts of generosity towards others. Jesus exhorted his disciples, 'Give, and it will be given to you. A good measure, pressed down, shaken together and running over, will be poured into your lap. For with the measure you use, it will be measured to you' (Luke 6:38).

Jesus' reply to James and John's audacious request was, 'You don't know what you are asking' (Mark 10:38). James wanted success and status, but Jesus knew that the way of discipleship prioritized relationship with God rather than any kind of reward.

Putting on the brakes

Like James and John, each one of us is on a journey with Jesus. He is travelling up to Jerusalem, but we may be diverted on to a downhill slope, unable to stop. We may have become focused upon ourselves in a way that forgets Jesus and ignores the needs of others. Our concentration might be so intently focused upon the problems of the slope that we forget that our best response is to put on the brakes.

There are some downhill runs that I will not attempt. Usually it is because they are too dangerous, and beyond my ability to negotiate. Experience has taught me that it is better to stop the bike before the descent becomes too perilous, and get off. Then I can push it back up the hill and find another route. Part of me feels a little deflated—I have missed the chance of another adrenalin rush—but the wiser part of me knows that I have saved myself from serious injury or even death.

By the grace of God, James learned that lesson of generosity and selflessness before it was too late. He put on the brakes and turned back just in time. He learned to give as well as to receive—even to the end, when he gave all that he had and was martyred for his faith (as we read in Acts 12:2).[49] Like James, we might have been on the road with Jesus for a long time. We might have listened to his teaching, been on the spiritual mountain-top, experienced his glory and even seen his miracles. Like James, we may nurture a secret selfishness that we manage to hide from everyone except God.

Travelling with Jesus on the way of the cross, we can be free. Even though sometimes it may be an uphill struggle, it can provide more life and freedom than a downhill freefall. As we move from greed to generosity, we have the chance to give to others and bless them. As we move from selfishness to selflessness, we can know the exhilaration of a full life with Christ.

Questions for reflection

1. What is the most frequent request that you make to Jesus?
2. Do you feel that there are some requests that Jesus does not allow? What are they?
3. What external influences (family, peer pressure, mass marketing) particularly affect you?

Mary Magdalene in the mire of dependency

Early on the first day of the week, while it was still dark, Mary Magdalene went to the tomb and saw that the stone had been removed from the entrance… Mary stood outside the tomb crying… she turned round and saw Jesus standing there, but she did not realize that it was Jesus. 'Woman,' he said, 'why are you crying? Who is it you are looking for?' Thinking he was the gardener, she said, 'Sir, if you have carried him away, tell me where you have put him, and I will get him.' Jesus said to her, 'Mary.' She turned towards him and cried out in Aramaic, 'Rabboni!' (which means Teacher). Jesus said, 'Do not hold on to me, for I have not yet returned to the Father. Go instead to my brothers and tell them, "I am returning to my Father and your Father, to my God and your God."' Mary Magdalene went to the disciples with the news: 'I have seen the Lord!' And she told them that he had said these things to her.

JOHN 20:1, 11A, 14–18

I had been a minister for nine months when I met Howard (not his real name). He was a family man with two children, and he was now unemployed. He was also an alcoholic. This was not uncommon where I worked, because there was a brewery in our parish. Many of the local people either worked there or had once worked there, and many of them had taken voluntary redundancy after becoming alcohol-dependent. This could be for a number of reasons, but the company did have very low prices in its social club and a very cheap 'seconds' shop. The church where I was working had a history of helping men like Howard to come off the booze and dry out. He was the first whom I was to help personally.

Howard was a good man. He was a friend of one of our regular church members and he had helped out from time to time with our youth club's football training. The alcoholism had taken its toll, though, and by the time I met him he was becoming too ill to attend training sessions. After spending some time with Howard and his wife, we talked through the possible options left to him. There was little prospect that he would be 'fast-tracked' for a liver transplant, and the drink was affecting his family and his marriage as well as his physical health. He had two choices: continue drinking so that the whole situation got worse, or seek help.

After much discussion, and not a little backtracking, he was finally persuaded to attend a Christian rehabilitation centre.[50] The church made sure that transport was provided for him, I promised that we would continue praying for him, and we left him there. Expecting to visit him in seven days' time, I was surprised to see him walking down the street 48 hours later. When I asked him why he was back, he confessed that he couldn't take the demands of the regime and had walked the ten miles home! When I said that walking ten miles was pretty demanding, he just shrugged his shoulders.

Reality check

Howard is just one, rather extreme example of someone who is dependent. We now live in a society that has become increasingly aware of the characteristics of the addict.[51] In 1980, there were ten residential addiction centres in the UK. In 2001, there were 150. In newsprint, the word 'addiction' was used 428 times in 1990; by 2000, this figure had risen dramatically to 11,707.[52] Our nation has, in fact, always had problems of dependency, whether through brewing, distillation, opium or other substances and techniques. With today's greater awareness of the issues, we may define dependency, or addiction, as the reliance 'upon any mood-altering substance, activity, belief, relationship or object'.[53]

Recent medical thinking has distinguished two basic categories of addiction: substance and process. Substance addictions usually involve the ingestion of something, with substances such as alcohol, cocaine and tobacco being three obvious examples. Process addictions involve dependency on a series of actions or interactions, such as shopping, physical exercise, gambling, work, relationships, sex, religious activities and even cleaning. Substance addictions tend to present more obvious signs of dependency, whereas process addictions can be more carefully hidden among the comings and goings of everyday life.

The word 'addiction' has serious overtones, and professionals in the field believe that it is used too variously. We will use the word 'dependency' rather than 'addiction' in this chapter to consider the ways in which we can rely unhealthily upon substances, people or routines. If we are honest, many of us are dependent upon, if not addicted to, a substance, person or activity. Some dependencies are more socially acceptable than others—coffee being one. The reason we depend upon these things is that they alter our mood. They can have physical effects—greater alertness, energy or relaxation—but they can also have an effect upon the emotions and personality. They can lead to compulsive behaviour and personal deterioration, and once the dependency is out of control, they are never enough. While we can control the power of some dependencies, the trouble begins when they start to control us. The more we depend upon the chosen obsession—be it a person, drug or habit—the more we need it. Like drinking sea water, the more we drink, the thirstier we become.

In order to understand how we become dependent, we need to understand the root of dependency. In his book *O Brave New Church: rescuing the addictive culture*, Mark Stibbe argues that the root cause of dependency is, in a word, pain. In today's climate, the bestselling products are pain relievers. And it is not just physical pain that can cause a dependency upon medication, but also emotional pain that we may be trying to numb. Unresolved emotional pain can lead to anxiety (a state of apprehension, tension and worry), panic (the onset of sudden inexplicable episodes of terror and a sense of impending doom), stress (a pattern of psychological and physiological responses that occur in difficult situations), or anger. These and other emotional responses can be suppressed by what we conventionally call drugs, or we may prefer to 'cope' with the pain by turning to temporary solutions such as addictive behaviours or substances. Sometimes, of course, we need to use prescribed medicines when experienced professionals reassure us that they will provide short-term respite. Patterns of addiction to Valium and barbiturates in recent decades, however, have shown that if they are taken for long periods, these medicines can lead to further problems. All too often in our society, pain is seen as something to be shunned or denied rather confronted and understood.

A surprising follower

When we think about the disciples of Jesus, we tend to think exclusively about the twelve men—the apostles—who followed Jesus. They were indeed central to his ministry, but it would be a mistake to limit our definition of a first-century disciple to this small inner group. Matthew's Gospel specifically mentions other followers (Matthew 8:19, 21) and John's Gospel alludes to a wider circle of disciples (John 10:24–27, 40–42). 'Following Jesus' was an expression that implied discipleship, but this 'following' could be manifested in either a figurative or physical form. We learn in John 19:38 that Joseph of Arimathea was a disciple of Jesus, although he does not seem to have physically followed Jesus. M.J. Wilkins describes the twin prerequisites of discipleship as paying the cost and committing yourself to the cause.[54] As such, disciples differed from the crowds that followed Jesus around the countryside, curious about his teaching and wanting his healing.

The Gospels and the book of Acts give a prominent place to the women who followed Jesus. While they were part of the wider group of disciples, some also followed Jesus during his travelling ministry. Luke tells us of a preaching tour when Jesus and the disciples were accompanied by women who were contributing to their support:

After this, Jesus travelled about from one town and village to another, proclaiming the good news of the kingdom of God. The Twelve were with him, and also some women who had been cured of evil spirits and diseases: Mary (called Magdalene) from whom seven demons had come out; Joanna the wife of Cuza, the manager of Herod's household; Susanna; and many others. These women were helping to support them out of their own means.
LUKE 8:1–3

This passage tells us that Mary Magdalene was one of the loyal band of followers who not only listened to Jesus' teaching but travelled around with him, serving his needs. In this respect, she fully demonstrates the commitment of a true disciple of Jesus, and her life has fascinated Christian tradition throughout the centuries.

Mary Magdalene has been variously described as a sinful woman or a prostitute. In addition, there have been many 'myths' that have grown up around her. Dan Brown's book *The Da Vinci Code* (Corgi, 2004), which supposes a marriage between Jesus and Mary Magdalene, has captured the coveted 'number one' sales spot throughout the world. In Martin Scorsese's film, *The Last Temptation of Christ* (1988), Jesus is tempted at his crucifixion by an alluring image of a peaceful and pleasant life with Mary Magdalene, enticing him to refuse the sacrifice he must make.

Many feminist theologians see Mary as a prime character in the church's marginalization of women over several centuries. The perception of Mary as a prostitute originated in AD591, when Pope Gregory the Great identified her with an unnamed sinful woman in

Luke 7. She then became known only for her alleged 'sin'. Almost 1400 years later, in 1969, the Church officially corrected its error, though it lingers in public consciousness.

Pope Gregory's mistake probably arose because of the position of the story of the anointing of Jesus in Luke 7:36–50, immediately preceding the naming of Mary as a disciple in Luke 8:2. If Mary were the same person as the 'sinful' woman who anointed Jesus, however, then would not Luke have made the connection explicit? In the 2004 film *The Passion of the Christ*, director and writer Mel Gibson makes a different connection. He equates Mary Magdalene with the woman caught in adultery (John 8:3–11).

All that we can be certain of is that Mary was delivered of some kind of possession (by 'seven demons', Luke 8:2), and that afterwards she used her resources to help Jesus' ministry. What these seven demons might have been is the basis of much conjecture. Does the number seven (the number of perfection in the Bible) signify a person who was thoroughly 'possessed' and now thoroughly delivered? Later Catholic theology equated the seven demons with the seven deadly sins of pride, lust, envy, anger, covetousness, gluttony and sloth, and suggested that in their place she was endued with corresponding virtues. Again, there is no basis in the Bible for such a colourful conclusion. In the film *The Miracle Maker* (2000), Murray Watts' screenplay portrays Mary Magdalene as having a 'disjointed' personality. Seven different voices are heard speaking to her and the confusion and pain on her face is clear even through the animation. This portrayal of Mary is hypothetical, yet it is a plausible reading of the text and shows an understanding of the New Testament culture and its view of demon possession.

However much conjecture there might be surrounding her background, we must not forget that Mary would have been confused and bewildered by her affliction, which would have led her to be ostracised from her community. She would have felt bereft of the support of family and friends, as well as being confused about what was reality and what was the influence of her waking nightmare. We know nothing about Jesus' deliverance of Mary Magdalene, although Mark 7:29, Matthew 8:32 and Luke 4:35 give us other examples of how he exercised this ministry. However it happened, her life would have been transformed. In short, Jesus had had an amazing effect upon her life. He had brought her healing, transformation and purpose.

Turmoil for Mary

Once again, Mary's world is turned upside down when Jesus is crucified. The man who had restored her life, brought the outcast in, and taught her to live again—her rabbi (teacher)—is gone. In our reading at the start of this chapter, we encounter her distraught with grief. Her despair is made worse by the indignity of a seeming graveyard theft: 'They have taken my Lord away... and I don't know where they have put him!' (John 20:13). Once again she is in the midst of pain, so bewildered by her agony that it blinds her to the amazing reality of that first Easter day. Her grief holds her captive as her former life of possession also held her captive, so she seeks the one thing that she knows will numb the pain and temper the loss that she feels. She asks for and looks for the dead body of the Messiah.

Mary returns to Jesus' burial place. All four of the Gospels (John 20:1; Matthew 28:1; Luke 24:1, 10; Mark 16:1) tell us that she went to visit the tomb, early in the morning. She had also been among the group of women who saw Jesus laid in the tomb on the evening of Good Friday. Now she comes across a man; one whom she cannot fully recognize, and thinks that he is the gardener (an apt mistake for the Son of God who created the whole universe!). She speaks to him, hoping that he may know something about the disappearance of the body.

Mary's problem here is one that all the disciples faced (Thomas exhibited this trait as well). Indeed, it is a problem that each one of us still faces: we do not hold a large enough view of Jesus. Mary was seeking a corpse instead of looking for a victorious, risen Lord. We too may have a view of Jesus that does not expect or sometimes even permit his transforming power in our lives. It may seem impossible that our sins can be forgiven because this man died upon a cross. It may sound just too easy to claim that we have eternal life because of his sacrifice.

To understand Mary Magdalene and her encounter with Jesus at the tomb, we need to engage our imagination, as well as taking care not to exaggerate the meaning of the text. Let's go over what we know about Mary. She is delivered from seven demons (presumably by Jesus, though this is not explicitly stated). She becomes a follower of Jesus, both by her change of attitude and her desire to follow him on his itinerant ministry. She is there at the crucifixion and the burial of Jesus, and is first at the tomb on the morning of the resurrection. Although there is no written evidence for it, it is quite likely that she and others would have been present at the last supper.

What do we know about Jesus? We know that he had com-passion upon all people, especially those that society branded as 'outcasts' (one example being his association with tax collectors and sinners, recorded in Mark 2:15). We know that he was comfortable associating with and touching those whom society shunned (see Luke 7:38, for example). Then, at the end of his encounter with Mary at the tomb, the risen Jesus says these curious words: 'Do not hold on to me, for I have not yet returned to the Father' (John 20:17). This is particularly striking because in the next few verses we read him saying to Thomas, 'Put your finger here; see my hands. Reach out your hand and put it into my side' (John 20:27). Why does Jesus ask Thomas to touch him and ask Mary not to do so? Is it because she is actually relating to him in a way that inhibits growth in faith, an unhelpfully dependent way?

In cultures and societies throughout the ages, women have been confined—and defined—within dependent relationships. Sometimes, it is true, economic and social circumstances meant that a dependent relationship was a necessity, but all too often it could be oppressive. The encounter at the tomb illustrates that Jesus does not seek a dependent relationship with Mary, or with any of his male followers either. Instead, he commissions her to go and tell the other disciples that he is 'returning to my Father and your Father, to my God and your God' (John 20:17). Jesus raises Mary's status to a messenger of the gospel—an apostle, literally 'one who is sent'—just as, later, he commissions his other followers to carry on his ministry. Paul develops this theme of our standing with Christ when he says, 'The Spirit himself testifies with our spirit that we are God's children. Now if we are children, then we are heirs—heirs of God and co-heirs with Christ' (Romans 8:16–17).

Is it possible to surmise that Mary Magdalene was romantically devoted to Jesus and expressed that devotion through her constant presence by his side? We could suggest that Mary is overly dependent upon the physical presence of Jesus. There is no biblical evidence that he showed favouritism towards Mary, although many minutes of cinematic screen action and literary pages have tended to focus upon this possibility.[55] Rather than abusing her love and trust, Jesus says, in response to Mary's dependency, 'Do not hold (cling) on to me' (John 20:17). She must release him and, in doing so, receive his salvation as the risen Christ. And Jesus does not leave any of his disciples desolate, but sends his Spirit to give them power: 'I will not leave you as orphans; I will come to you' (John 14:18); 'And I will ask the Father, and he will give you another Counsellor to be with you for ever' (John 14:16).

If there is any kind of dependent relationship for Jesus, it must be his relationship with his heavenly Father: 'I am returning to my Father and your Father, to my God and your God' (John 20:17). The word 'dependent' here is inappropriate, however. A more accurate description of the Father–Son relationship might be *inter*dependent. Our culture encourages people to rebel against the paternalism and maternalism of our past. The more structured life of past decades has been rejected and replaced instead by a false sense of the supremacy of the self. Much advertising exhorts us to live independent lives, free from any sense of responsibility. One slogan that encapsulates this philosophy is 'Just do it.' The search for freedom and independence has led to a greater sense of isolation within communities, however.

Some people are literally isolated from others and suffer from loneliness. Some feel emotionally isolated through broken relationships. Instead of striving for independence, and suffering from isolation, humankind is made to strive after interdependence in the image of God—Father, Son and Holy Spirit. God is trinitarian and mutually interdependent.

God's answer to dependency

In recent years, theologians have been considering how a trinitarian view of God, as Father, Son and Holy Spirit, should impact the way Christians see themselves; both as individuals and as communities. They wrestle with the mind-bending concept that God is one and yet three persons—one substance, yet three distinct identities.

One concept that has been used to express the dynamic relationship between Father, Son and Holy Spirit is that of a dance. This idea presents a model of the Trinity as a dynamic community of relationship in which we are invited to participate. The interweaving of the persons of the Trinity shows their intimate relationship with one another, and as co-heirs with Christ we are drawn into that intimacy. The words used to describe the relationship from the days of the earliest creeds are that the Son 'indwells' the Father, the Father 'contains' the Son, and the Spirit 'fills' the Father.[56]

We proclaim the Church's faith in Jesus Christ.
We believe and declare that our Lord Jesus Christ,
the Son of God, is both divine and human.

God, of the being of the Father,
the only Son from before time began;
human from the being of his mother, born in the world;
fully God and fully human;
human in both mind and body.

As God he is equal to the Father,
as human he is less than the Father.
Although he is both divine and human
he is not two beings but one Christ.

One, not by turning God into flesh,
but by taking humanity into God;
truly one, not by mixing humanity with Godhead,
but by being one person.[57]

This credal statement expresses the interdependence of the Trinity. Each person relies upon another to fulfil the work of salvation—saving and freeing humankind from sin. The Father relies upon the Son taking on human flesh. This is the idea of God's self-emptying that we read of in Philippians 2:6–7: 'Who, being in very nature God, did not consider equality with God something to be grasped, but made himself nothing, taking the very nature of a servant, being made in human likeness'. The Son relies upon the Father, as we read in Jesus' words in John's Gospel: 'I tell you the truth, the Son can do nothing by himself; he can do only what he sees his Father doing, because whatever the Father does the Son also does' (John 5:19). The Spirit empowers the Son: 'Jesus returned to Galilee in the power of the Spirit, and news about him spread through the whole countryside' (Luke 4:14). The 'dance' of interdependence continues as the work of the Holy Spirit is seen in the lives of believers such as Mary Magdalene and generations of Christians up to the present day.

The 'dance' of the Trinity draws us into its circle and includes us into the life of God. James Houston puts it this way:

This presence of God within us makes us more human, more personal and more individuated as such, as well as more life-giving and sharing with others, when consciously and deliberately responded to by us. We are given by the 'giving God' the grace to be, to relate, and to give of ourselves. This is what it means to live in a godly way.[58]

This view of God as Trinity is a challenge to 'the modern cult of the individual, [and] it teaches us to think in terms of complex webs of mutuality and participation'.[59] We are 'our brother's keeper' (Genesis 4:9) and the challenge of interdependency means that we need to support and encourage others in our society to experience the joy of community with one another and with God. In very practical ways, that may mean establishing local networks of relationships where people can give and receive support on issues as diverse as employment, family life, finance and mobility. The paradox within the heart of God is that it is in self-giving that we find fulfilment, in sacrifice and commitment that we receive blessing.

Everything is not lost

Like Mary, many of us come to Jesus with a history of dependence. To put it in today's terms, we come 'with a lot of baggage', which we carry into our Christian life. We may only notice this when we are a little way into the journey, after having taken a significant step of faith. Areas of dependence can also ensnare Christians who make the mistake of thinking that they are 'sorted out' as disciples. As we considered in the story of Matthew, destructive habits and lifestyles often begin almost by accident. We think that we can justify buying one more product (another pair of shoes, for example), or spending a little bit longer with a colleague when we should be on our way home. We think that we can always log off that website, leave that drink or stub out that cigarette. Then we begin to find that we cannot: we leave it for a short while but return later—secretly.

Recovery groups are available for all kinds of addictions. What the Christian approach does is to take this tool and invest it with a Christ-centred theology, as opposed to a more general acknowledgment of our need for a higher power to release us from ourselves. Many churches are recognizing underlying dependency and turning to different teaching programmes that can offer help. This all points to an increased recognition that, despite having made a significant step of faith, Christians may still be struggling with a number of issues from which, in the past, people may have expected them to be automatically 'set free'.

Like Mary, we often remain blind to our dependence. The risen saviour who stood before Mary stands before us. We cling to our pain and dependence—whatever that substance, habit or person may be—and still Jesus doesn't give up on us. He asks, 'Why are you crying? Who is it you are looking for?' (John 20:15). This is an expression of great concern and love from the Son of God, not only to Mary but to each one of us. Mary was looking for a body: she was depending upon a physical presence to offer her a little comfort in her desolation. She never dreamed that Jesus would rise from the dead and that he would call her by name and remake her world, just as this same risen Lord calls us by name and will remake our world if we let him.

We may all go through the experience of unhelpful dependency at some point in our lives. It may be a socially acceptable dependency that only we know about—or one or two very close friends as well. Like Mary, we may have experienced pain and found something or someone that anaesthetizes that pain, when perhaps it would be better to acknowledge that we are hurt and look for healing. Whatever our circumstances, Jesus comes to us as he came to Mary.

If Mary's story is like ours, Jesus tells us, 'Do not hold on' to your pain any longer, but 'go instead'. We can go and live a life set free from that captivity; go instead and tell others of the freedom that Jesus can give; go instead and live a risen life! The amazing truth about the Christian life is that God chooses to live a life of inter-dependence with us. He chooses to partner us in the dance of creativity and the work of mission. Mary showed the depth of her commitment to being a disciple of Christ by obediently answering the call to let go—and go out to tell others.

Howard, the man in the story at the beginning of this chapter, walked away. He walked away from a tough decision that, while it would not have made for an easy life, would have made for wholeness and healing eventually. He walked back into a life of alcohol-dependence and pain. Whatever our story—and it may be not be as grim as Howard's—we too have a choice. We can listen to the words of Jesus and follow his call, or we can walk away. Only one of those choices offers joy and peace that words cannot express.

Questions for reflection

1. Who or what are you secretly dependent upon?
2. What excuses do you subconsciously give to justify that dependency?
3. What do you think that Jesus might say if you were to tell him about that dependency?

Peter: crashed and burned!

'You are not one of his disciples, are you?' the girl at the door asked Peter. He replied, 'I am not.' It was cold, and the servants and officials stood around a fire they had made to keep warm. Peter also was standing with them, warming himself... As Simon Peter stood warming himself, he was asked, 'You are not one of his disciples, are you?' He denied it, saying, 'I am not.' One of the high priest's servants, a relative of the man whose ear Peter had cut off, challenged him, 'Didn't I see you with him in the olive grove?' Again Peter denied it, and at that moment a rooster began to crow...

When they had finished eating, Jesus said to Simon Peter, 'Simon son of John, do you truly love me more than these?' 'Yes, Lord,' he said, 'you know that I love you.' Jesus said, 'Feed my lambs.' Again Jesus said, 'Simon son of John, do you truly love me?' He answered, 'Yes, Lord, you know that I love you.' Jesus said, 'Take care of my sheep.' The third time he said to him, 'Simon son of John, do you love me?' Peter was hurt because Jesus asked him the third time, 'Do you love me?' He said, 'Lord, you know all things; you know that I love you.' Jesus said, 'Feed my sheep.'

JOHN 18:17–18, 25–27; 21:15–17

'No one likes a failure.' So the saying goes—except that we've all been a 'failure'. To put it more accurately, we have all failed at one time or another. (We'll explore the important difference between failing and being 'a failure' later in the chapter.) How does Jesus react to disciples who fail? How should we react to failure in our own life? This is an important hill on our journey that we need to climb.

'Crashed and burnt', 'wiped out', 'totalled': these expressions (and a few more that are unprintable) describe what happens when a mountain bike rider comes off at high speed. Thankfully, it hasn't happened to me too often, especially when I've been out riding alone (mobile phones don't always work very well in the middle of nowhere). I have experienced disaster while riding, however, and I didn't like it, so I made a plan to avoid it in future. Near my house is a mountain biking centre where the national championships are held. As you can imagine, there is some very challenging terrain, most of which is beyond my present abilities to ride. So I decided to receive some instruction. Two friends and I struggled under the demands of our young instructor, who seemed to make everything look very easy. I was invited to tackle a particularly tricky downhill section through a tangle of protruding tree roots. Time and again, I fell off, or 'bottled out'. Feeling an increasing sense of frustration and beginning to look a fool, I said, 'Right, I'll give it one last try.' 'No,' I was told by my young instructor, 'you won't give it one last try. We never say that we are going to give a jump or a trick or a skill one last try. You'll give it one more try.'

Peter's journey to faith

Peter is another of Jesus' disciples who is allowed one more try. He is a larger-than-life character in the Bible. As we read the Gospel accounts of his exploits, we are able to picture him better than any of the other disciples. (My image of him is as a big man, fully bearded, barrel-chested, with a quick temper but also with a ready laugh.) He must have made an impression upon the Gospel writers Matthew, Mark, Luke and John, because he plays a central part in all of their narratives. There must also have been something special about Peter that Jesus saw, because he was to become one of Jesus' closest friends and followers. In his letters to the churches, Peter refers to this close relationship with Jesus when he says, 'We did not follow cleverly invented stories when we told you about the power and coming of our Lord Jesus Christ, but we were eyewitnesses of his majesty' (2 Peter 1:16). Peter had first-hand experience of Jesus' ministry.

His discipleship journey begins when his brother Andrew brings him to meet Jesus (John 1:41). Luke's account introduces a very interesting detail into the early part of their relationship. It would seem from Luke's Gospel that Peter already knows who Jesus is, because Jesus has met and spoken to him when he visited his house and healed his mother-in-law (Luke 4:38–39). When Jesus is walking by the lake, he sees the crowds gathering around him and he asks to borrow a boat from Peter, who is mending his nets. Jesus asks him to put the boat out a little way from the shore. (We can imagine Peter getting in the boat to do this, so making him a captive audience to Jesus' message.) After the teaching of the crowd is concluded, Jesus invites Peter to go fishing. Somewhat reluctantly, he agrees and is miraculously rewarded by a huge catch of fish.

In Peter's response, we see something of the character of the man. He does not say, 'Why didn't I know where the fish were?' Rather, his response is of a man who is in the presence of the divine: 'When Simon Peter saw this, he fell at Jesus' knees and said, "Go away from me, Lord; I am a sinful man!"' (Luke 5:8). His words carry echoes of Isaiah, when he says, 'Woe to me! I am ruined! For I am a man of unclean lips, and I live among a people of unclean lips, and my eyes have seen the King, the Lord Almighty' (Isaiah 6:5).

Simon Peter is not being critical of his fishing skills; he is being critical of his life! He is a 'sinful man' and exhibits a spiritual awareness that shows him to be both insightful and humble. He is someone who can see, with the eyes of faith, things that others cannot see, but he can also recognize his own unworthiness. These two character traits make Peter a natural friend of Jesus.

Peter shows other qualities of faith in the famous story about

Jesus walking upon the water. Jesus and his disciples are seeking a solitary place, away from the crowds and safe from the murderous Herod (who has just beheaded John the Baptist). After Jesus has fed the five thousand (Matthew 14:13–21), his disciples go on ahead to the other side of Lake Galilee, while Jesus comes along later. The manner of Jesus' transport across the lake puts the fear of God into the disciples: 'During the fourth watch of the night Jesus went out to them, walking on the lake' (Matthew 14:25). It is Peter alone who has the courage to call out to Jesus, and he is the only one who displays the courage to step out of the relative safety and comfort of the boat and take the huge first step on to the water. John Ortberg reflects upon some of the emotions that Peter might have been feeling at the time:

I can't believe it. Nobody thought I'd actually get out of the boat—I didn't think I'd do it myself. When I let go of the side, it was the hardest thing I've ever done. I was afraid I'd die. Now I find myself actually doing what Jesus is doing. I don't know how it's working—I'm not walking any differently. Yet something—Someone—is holding me up. I think I'm beginning to understand now. It is true. He really is the One.[60]

However we might understand this miraculous story, at the heart of it is Peter putting his trust in Jesus in a new and profound way. As the story goes on to tell, Peter 'saw the wind', and 'he was afraid' (14:30). His trust could only last so long, but still he shows a level of faith—both here and at other times—that Jesus applauds, saying that on such faith and trust 'I will build my church, and the gates of Hades will not overcome it' (Matthew 16:18). Peter's humility, insight and trust are three reasons why Jesus chose him to be part of his inner circle of disciples, and his personal qualities made him stand out as one of the key leaders of the early Church.

The cracks begin to show

After having made a good start on the path, Peter begins to show that his faith in Christ is more brittle than it would first appear. A crowning moment in their relationship comes when Peter testifies to Christ's lordship (though this is sadly undone soon after). The disciples have escaped to be on their own, leaving behind the crowds and the questions of the Pharisees and Sadducees. In a quiet moment, Jesus asks them to reflect upon all the religious specu-lation that they have heard about him. Now it is the disciples' turn to decide: 'When Jesus came to the region of Caesarea Philippi, he asked his disciples, "Who do people say the Son of Man is?"' (Matthew 16:13). They ponder the different views that have been expressed: some consider Jesus to be a prophet—another fore-runner who, like John the Baptist, will prepare the way for the coming Messiah.

Peter is not willing to base his response on the opinions of others, however. Rather, he speaks confidently about something that may have been just a shadow of a thought until that moment: 'You are the Christ, the Son of the living God' (Matthew 16:16). Jesus affirms Peter's openness to God and then goes on to explain how the Christ must suffer many things, that he must be killed and on the third day be raised to life. Soon after this, Peter makes a significant misjudgment. We don't know exactly how soon after his confident proclamation that this happened, but three of the Gospel writers link the two stories together. Hearing about the suffering of the Messiah, Peter rebukes Jesus and rejects the path that Jesus says he must take: '"Never, Lord!" he said. "This shall never happen to you!"' (Matthew 16:22). Peter's strong will, linked to his ignorance, produces a shocking bit of arrogance. He confesses that Jesus is the Messiah and then speaks in a way that implies he knows more of God's will than the Messiah himself.

Peter's arrogance shows itself in a second error of judgment when he engages Jesus in another theological discussion. Jesus has been explaining to his followers how they should resolve issues of conflict among themselves. He gives them a threefold strategy. If someone sins against you, first you must go and show the person their fault privately. Second, if that does not work, you are to seek arbitration with the help of another individual. Third, if that still does not work, you should seek the help of the Christian community. In the light of Jesus' teaching on sin and forgiveness, Peter poses a question: 'Lord, how many times shall I forgive my brother when he sins against me? Up to seven times?' (Matthew18:21).

Peters' choice of the number seven betrays an attitude of spiritual pride. In discussion among rabbis, the consensus was that a Jew might be forgiven a repeated sin three times; on the fourth offence, there should be no forgiveness. Peter, thinking himself generous-hearted, volunteers 'seven times' in answer to his own question. This is, of course, a significantly larger number than the consensus, showing him in a charitable light. The number seven also had significance to Jews as a complete or 'round number'. Jesus knows Peter's heart, though, and uses the opportunity to explain to the disciples that they should demonstrate the unlimited grace of God in their human relationships. Just as God forgives us beyond what we deserve, our forgiveness of others cannot possibly be limited by frequency or quantity.

Just as cracks in a perishing tyre don't mean that it will burst immediately, but that it will be vulnerable to increased pressure, so Peter is beginning to demonstrate a spiritual overconfidence in his own abilities. Later on, the pressure will become too much.

The third example of Peter's arrogance or overconfidence is at the last supper. Throughout his ministry Jesus had modelled to his followers the meaning of servant leadership. At this last meal he reinforced the importance of self-giving love by washing the disciples' feet. The Jewish custom was that at the celebration of a special meal, guests would be welcomed by servants at the door. The lowliest of the servants would be assigned the task of removing the guests' sandals and washing their feet. Could Jesus have asked one of the other disciples to do this on his behalf? If any of them had accepted, it could have been seen as an admission of inferiority in front of their peers. So, instead of asking one of his followers, sometime during the meal Jesus rose, removed his outer cloak, tied a towel around his waist, and began to perform the work of the servant who was not present. It was an act of voluntary humiliation.

Peter spoke his own mind very strongly at this point: 'No, you shall never wash my feet' (John 13:8). The force of this assertion is worth clarifying. The use of the word 'no' and 'never' imply 'never in all eternity shall you wash my feet'. Peter's words reveal both his impetuosity and his high regard for Jesus, yet his attitude that Jesus should not degrade himself by assuming such a position betray his continued lack of understanding. Jesus' reply expresses his purpose: 'Unless I wash you, you have no part with me' (John 13:8b). It is necessary to make Peter clean for the dinner, but his personality also needs cleansing to make him fit for the kingdom of God. The external washing was intended to be a picture of spiritual washing from evil. Peter still does not grasp the deeper significance of the action as he then asks to be washed from head to toe: 'Not just my feet but my hands and my head as well!' (v. 9).

Peter is a complex mixture of openness, humility and trust, while at the same time showing himself to be arrogant, proud and over-confident. This potent mix of character traits makes his later denial of Jesus all the more important for us to understand, as we too can demonstrate spiritual responses akin to Peter's.

Acknowledging failure

When Winston Churchill was asked to identify one of the most significant events in his life, which had made him the leader he was, he is said to have answered, 'When I failed end-of-year exams at school and had to stay in that year until I passed them.' As we have already reflected, no one likes to fail, but it is what we do with failure that matters. 'If you want to be successful you don't study people who have been a failure,' says Bob Schwartz, the self-help guru of the 1990s. In fact, quite the opposite is true. Considering how Peter faced failure can help us in our response to it.

At this moment in Peter's story, we need to consider how Jesus would have been viewed at the time of his arrest. Jesus' capture, arrest and night-time interrogation would have been seen by many as a humiliating failure of his ministry. We should remember that he had entered Jerusalem triumphantly on what we call Palm Sunday. Only days later, he was arrested and tried, jeered by the crowds, tortured and executed by the Romans under the gaze of the religious authorities. Although Peter might have imagined the severity of the outcome of Jesus' capture, the fact was that he was connected with a maverick religious leader who seemed to have failed in his mission to usher in the kingdom of God.

Following after Jesus, who has been led away from the garden of Gethsemane by armed guards, Peter cautiously enters the courtyard of the high priest. He is challenged by a servant girl and his reply displays a range of typical responses to failure, encapsulating many of the emotions that we may feel at such a time. '"You are not one of his disciples, are you?" the girl at the door asked Peter. He replied, "I am not"' (John 18:17). First he denies association with Jesus, unwilling to be linked to someone being investigated for heresy. Psychologists describe denial as a defence mechanism that rejects personal responsibility for one's own words or actions.

Luke's Gospel tells us that the servant girl 'looked closely at him and said, "This man was with him"' (Luke 22:56). This would have engendered a second emotional response in Peter: fear. He might have felt particularly fearful as he had been implicated in a violent attack earlier: 'One of the high priest's servants, a relative of the man whose ear Peter had cut off, challenged him, "Didn't I see you with [Jesus] in the olive grove?"' (John 18:26). When we have failed, or are connected with someone who has failed, we often find ourselves paralysed by fear. As hard as it can be, we do better to own up to our part in the event honestly—both to God and to others. Although we might be tempted to do and say nothing in the face of failure, that is rarely the right response. We need to confront our fear at the moment of failure and admit it to God and others. In addition, we need to reflect upon the episode later, so that we might take action and avoid it happening again. That way, we learn properly from our mistakes. Peter took an opposite course of action. When he was posed with a question that invited a further denial of Christ, he took it: 'As Simon Peter stood warming himself, he was asked, "You are not one of his disciples, are you?" He denied it, saying, "I am not"' (John 18:25).

A third response that can arise from a sense of failure is a desire to blame someone else. The third time that Peter was questioned about Jesus, Mark's Gospel tells us, 'He began to call down curses on himself, and he swore to them, "I don't know this man you're talking about"' (Mark 14:71). Although the calling down of curses might sound as if Peter is taking personal responsibility for his own words, he uses the religious language to turn the accuser's attention from himself and on to God. Peter might have been expecting the curse to take the form of a thunder crack or a lightning bolt. Instead, he heard the sound of the cock crowing and remembered Jesus' words: '"Before the rooster crows twice you will disown me three times." And he broke down and wept' (Mark 14:72). Now Peter demonstrates a fourth response to failure: a deep sense of shame. Shame follows a person's realization that he or she has failed to meet his or her ideals of expectations. As with Peter, the shame of failure often brings out a strong emotional response.

As we have said, failure comes to us all and presents each one of us with a challenge: how will we respond to its pain? Peter demonstrated a variety of negative responses to failure that finally led to the realization of his own pride and weakness. The bitter tears of shame would eventually lead him to the point of restoration. Before he could arrive at that point, however, he had to experience the trauma of Good Friday and Jesus' crucifixion.

Receiving restoration

I asked God for strength, that I might achieve,
I was made weak, that I might learn humbly to obey.

I asked God for health, that I might do greater things,
I was given infirmity, that I might do better things.

I asked for riches, that I might be happy,
I was given poverty, that I might be wise.

I asked for power, that I might have the praise of men,
I was given weakness, that I might feel the need of God.

I asked for all things, that I might enjoy life,
I was given life, that I might enjoy all things.

I got nothing that I asked for—but everything I had hoped for.

Almost despite myself, my unspoken prayers were answered.
I am among men, most richly blessed.[61]

Restoration after failure can come in surprising ways. As this anonymous poem suggests, and to paraphrase Mick Jagger, you don't always get what you want, but you get what you need! John's Gospel alone includes the restoration of Peter, and it takes the form of an epilogue to the Gospel account, reading like a reminiscence— an eyewitness account of a very personal encounter.

This encounter with Jesus enables restoration and commissioning for Peter in a somewhat surprising way. Seven disciples have decided to go fishing and Jesus comes to the shore. He calls out to them and invites the fishermen to throw their nets out on the right side of the boat, where they will find some fish. They do so, and catch a large haul (153 fish, John 21:11).

After Jesus has shared breakfast with the disciples, he turns his attention to Peter: 'When they had finished eating, Jesus said to Simon Peter, "Simon son of John, do you truly love me more than these?" "Yes, Lord," he said, "you know that I love you"' (John 21:15). There is much scholarly debate about the words used between Jesus and Peter. The word 'love' in Greek can come in four different forms. In this conversation between Peter and Jesus, Peter uses one form, *phileo* (meaning to love 'fondly', or 'as a friend'), but Jesus first uses another form, *agapé* (meaning 'divine, self-giving love'). Some scholars argue that as Jesus asks the question a third time, he adopts Peter's word for love (*phileo*), acknowledging Peter's inability to speak in terms of divine self-giving love, but not rejecting him because of it. Whether this linguistic detail was uppermost in Jesus' mind during the conversation is in some doubt, especially if Peter and Jesus were speaking in Aramaic on the shore, a language without the same variety of words for 'love'! Something more important is going on.

True restoration requires an acknowledgment of failure. Over recent years in South Africa, the Truth and Reconciliation Commission has been bringing together the victims and perpetrators of violence. In the UK, the 'restorative justice' programme has been bringing together victims and perpetrators of crime. In each case, it is believed to be helpful and healing for a face-to-face confession of 'sin' to take place. In a similar way, the dialogue between Peter and Jesus confronts the disciple's failure face to face, but in a gentle and compassionate way. Jesus seems to recognize Peter's attachment to him, even when he questions his ability to love at all costs: 'Again Jesus said, "Simon son of John, do you truly love me?" He answered, "Yes, Lord, you know that I love you"' (John 21:16). The threefold denial of Peter is echoed by the threefold question of Jesus. 'Peter was hurt because Jesus asked him the third time' (v. 17), yet this threefold question served both as an acknowledgment of past failure and an opportunity for repentance. Failure gives Peter (and us) the opportunity to acknowledge to Jesus that we are loved, despite our failure. If our relationship with God is based purely upon successes, it will only last as long as those moments of transitory glory. When we realize, deep down, that Jesus comes to us even in the moments after denial and still loves us in our failure, then we realize that we are held by a God who is stronger than success or failure.

Commissioned for a task

Paradoxically, failure can be a gift from God. God will never use failure for our discouragement. Instead, he will use it to enable our recommissioning for service. Very often, however, failure in Christian life and ministry does not lead to recommissioning for service, but to 'burnout'. One tragic example of this was Evan Roberts, leader of the 1904 Welsh revival.

From the middle of the 19th century to the middle of the 20th, Wales experienced many major spiritual revivals, the greatest of which began in 1904. Part of the widespread public appeal of the revival lay in Evan Roberts himself, a charismatic and sincere preacher. He acted as the public face of the religious leadership. Meetings led by Roberts would be a mixture of prayer, self-examination and singing, and they could last for hours. His mission was closely followed by the local and national press, and Roberts became something of a personality, with his picture regularly in the papers as well as being featured on postcards. In today's terms he might have been labelled a 'spiritual David Beckham'.[62] By the middle of 1905, the revival was all but over and Roberts left Wales for a number of years, his ministry burnt out after a few short months. Broken in health, he retired from public view for the remaining half-century of his life. This could well be described as the tragic story of a life only half lived.

The attitude that Jesus displays to Peter can reassure us that we always have a second chance. God may call us to a different kind of ministry, but he always invites us again into his service and into his family. Jesus probed Peter's sincerity and commitment by asking the same question three times, and each time Peter replied, Jesus commissioned him to a task. The nuances of Jesus' commission are quite subtle, and once again we should take care not to read too much into them. In John 21:15, he says, 'Feed (pasture) my lambs', in verse 16, 'Take care of (shepherd) my sheep', and again in verse 17, 'Feed (pasture) my sheep.'

In literal terms, pasturing the sheep involved simply taking them to the right place where good food could be found, while shepherding implies the greater care and guardianship that a shepherd exercises. This threefold calling does not give Peter the sole responsibility for the oversight of Christ's followers; all of Jesus' spiritually mature disciples were called to be shepherds. Peter recognizes this himself when he later writes, 'Be shepherds of God's flock that is under your care, serving as overseers' (1 Peter 5:2), but this new challenge to Peter demands a total renewal of his loyalty to Jesus as he restates Peter's responsibilities.

Jesus is not bestowing a position of authority upon Peter; he is giving him a task. As Don Carson says, 'This ministry is described in verbs, not nouns.'[63] It is a helpful reminder that if we judge success in terms of positions held, we will more easily succumb to failure. If we join in the service of Christ and do his bidding, then regardless of rank, we will experience Christ's rewards.

Peter's letters to the churches can give us a glimpse into the life of a man who has been through failure and come out the other side. They show a man who speaks with humility, and empathizes with the struggles and challenges of living as a follower of Christ. In one section of his letters, we get a real insight into how Jesus' new commission has shaped his life and ministry:

To the elders among you, I appeal as a fellow elder, a witness of Christ's sufferings and one who also will share in the glory to be revealed: Be shepherds of God's flock that is under your care, serving as overseers—not because you must, but because you are willing, as God wants you to be; not greedy for money, but eager to serve; not lording it over those entrusted to you, but being examples to the flock.
1 PETER 5:1–3

The basis of Peter's appeal to the elders is threefold. Firstly, he is a fellow elder. He has been charged, as they have, to take care of Christ's 'flock'. Secondly, he encourages a spirit of willing service among those who lead, and discourages reluctant compliance. He also encourages an attitude of humility towards those in the church community, such that the leader does not assume a position of power and control. In summary, Peter's letters indicate that his arrogance, pride and overconfidence have gone, and in their place are humility, generosity of spirit and a heart of service. His recommissioning for service is complete and he can truly fulfil his vow, made long ago to Jesus: 'Even if I have to die with you, I will never disown you' (Mark 14:31).

As we have seen, Jesus never writes anyone off as a 'failure'. Yes, all have sinned and fallen short of the glory of God (Romans 3:23), but it is in God's character to have mercy, to restore and re-commission us for service. Our success-driven culture might frown upon those who have failed, and write them off. Jesus doesn't do this, and neither should his followers. We are often hardest upon ourselves in this regard. As we look over our lives, each one of us can remember times when we have denied Christ, disowned his followers or turned away from God. We may feel that God cannot use us after such a failure and, whether physically or not, like Peter we weep bitterly. We often echo the sentiment of my frustration at the mountain bike centre: 'Well, I've given it one last try. That's it for me, I'm done.' We feel that we are 'done' with Christianity, and Jesus is 'done' with us. He is not, and the wisdom of my young biking instructor could almost have echoed down the centuries from the lips of Jesus himself. We can give it one more try, and if that doesn't work out, still another one after that! God is not just the God of the second chance, but of the third, fourth, fifth, even the one hundreth chance! Peter learned that for himself and lived a 'resurrection' life, and we can as well!

Questions for reflection

1. Peter demonstrates the traits of insight, humility and trust. Which of these would you most like to develop in the coming months? Why?
2. If Jesus was going to cleanse you and wash your feet, what character flaw would you ask him to wash away?
3. Have you ever considered yourself a 'failure' when really you have just failed? What lessons from Peter's encounter with Jesus should you apply to your own experience?

The next hill

There is a viewing point near my house. After a brisk walk, a cycle ride, or even a lazy drive, you can stand and look over the skyline of London. All the main landmarks are visible. You can see the London Eye, the St Mary Axe building (or 'Gherkin', as it is better known) and others too. From this hill you can see across a sweeping panorama of humanity and industry. Most of the sites are more than 20 miles away, and yet they are clearly visible. That is the wonder of hills. They provide you with perspective, and when you reach the top of them, you can know the satisfaction of looking back and remembering what it took to get there. The challenge, of course, is that you only see the full view when you have reached the top!

In the last few chapters we have considered some obstacles on the discipleship path. We have thought about those 'hills' that challenge us on the Christian journey. Each obstacle has been summarized by a word that resonates with our culture: doubt, decision, opportunity, selfishness, dependency and failure. Each chapter has examined the life of a New Testament disciple of Jesus who faced this 'hill' or challenge. As we considered the disciple, we have also been able to look at how Jesus helped them to tackle their 'hill' and overcome it.

I believe that we can take great strength from the fact that the first disciples of Jesus struggled and overcame their obstacles. As they heard Jesus' words or saw his example, they could acknowledge where they had fallen and why they needed to pick themselves up. Jesus spoke words of challenge, encouragement, rebuke or affirmation to help them on their way, so that they were able to tackle the next 'hill' and get a new perspective on their lives. Jesus helped them to stand above their problems and see further than they could before.

Fellow travellers

Jesus helped Thomas not to be side-tracked by doubt. He came to Thomas, knowing his personality, and spoke words of challenge and faith into his life. He enabled Thomas to see that his limited worldview was not large enough to include the resurrection of God's Son. Through this encounter, Thomas was drawn back into the community from which he had separated himself. Dynamic faith and action replaced paralysing doubt in Thomas' life.

Jesus met with Andrew and offered him a new way of life. Andrew's life was lived in the shadow of his brother, Peter, but Jesus spoke directly to him and asked him, 'What do you want from your life?' (in effect, 'How would you like your life to be different?'). He instilled worth in Andrew and taught him the value of being with Jesus on the journey. He took Andrew's innate ability to invite people and include them in God's journey, and released him into a new way of life. Jesus helped Andrew on to the road and up the next hill.

Levi had pledged his life to money, and to social and spiritual isolation. He had made a box (or booth) for himself and could not find a way out. Jesus stood at the intersection of Levi's life and said, 'Choose: follow me.' The real option of staying in his job and his social sphere, and maintaining his financial security, must have been a genuine consideration for Levi, but he chose the challenge of a different hill and followed Jesus. With that choice came a new name—Matthew, 'gift of God'.

James had to confront his own selfishness. His life was heading in a downward direction and Jesus' words forced him to stop. He turned his attitudes around after the resurrection appearances of Jesus, and gave his life for Christ.

Mary Magdalene also had a defining moment in her spiritual journey. She moved from dependence upon to interdependence with Jesus. She learned that it was better to 'go and tell' than it was to 'hold on'.

Our final chapter considered Peter. He thought of himself as a failure, the one who denied Jesus even though he had claimed that he would die for him. Peter showed his responses to failure as he spoke with his accusers in the high priest's courtyard. He had to be willing to give his journey with Jesus 'one more try'. Jesus gently confronted him with his failures, thereby giving him a chance to start again. Peter may have 'crashed', but his life was not a write-off. God had new adventures for him to begin.

Whether we are at the beginning of our spiritual journey, like Levi, or whether we feel that our discipleship has come to an end, like Peter, Thomas and Mary, Jesus can help us to overcome the difficulties that inhibit our journey with him. It is worth acknowledging that we have considered only a few obstacles on the path of discipleship, and there are many others that we might have addressed. Nevertheless, we can learn important lessons about our own pilgrimage from these six followers of Christ. In a lifetime's journey with Jesus, we need to remember that there will always be another hill to overcome. We will never fully surmount every obstacle until we finally see God face to face. Then, and only then, 'every valley shall be raised up, every mountain and hill made low; the rough ground shall become level, the rugged places a plain. And the glory of the Lord will be revealed, and all mankind together will see it' (Isaiah 40:4–5). Until that time we must be ready to confront the obstacles in our path with the strength that Jesus can give.

If obstacles on the journey are an intrinsic part of 'the Way' (early Christians were called followers of 'The Way' in Acts 24:14 and elsewhere), how can we best tackle them?

Hills are opportunities, not obstacles

Hills are actually opportunities, not obstacles. Having described the hills that the disciples faced as obstacles, it is worth reconsidering their role in the Christian life. If the challenges of the Christian life are seen only in a negative way, we will become demotivated and discouraged. If, instead, we see times of struggle as character-forming, we will come to each difficulty with a greater inner resourcefulness. Clearly this is easy to say when life is going well and harder to acknowledge when we are struggling to reach the 'summit'. That is why it is important to reconsider our view of the Christian life before we face another difficulty. Then we will feel better able to surmount it.

When Jesus spoke his famous last words, known as the great commission, I do not think it was any accident that he said them on a hill:

Then the eleven disciples went to Galilee, to the mountain where Jesus had told them to go. When they saw him, they worshipped him; but some doubted. Then Jesus came to them and said, 'All authority in heaven and on earth has been given to me. Therefore go and make disciples of all nations, baptizing them in the name of the Father and of the Son and of the Holy Spirit, and teaching them to obey everything I have commanded you. And surely I am with you always, to the very end of the age.'
MATTHEW 28:16–20

In that moment, Jesus widened the disciples' vision of what was possible. He was opening their eyes to a new vision of God's kingdom, beyond being a Galilean religious sect. That kingdom would involve all nations, and it was to be initiated by God's Spirit at work in them! Jesus was not painting a picture of a dark and difficult future, although he had spoken to them honestly of such difficulties before ('If the world hates you, keep in mind that it hated me first', John 15:18). He was telling them of opportunities, not obstacles.

This does not mean that we offer false hopes of an easy, carefree life for Christians. Instead, we can acknowledge the struggles and turn them to our advantage. As Paul wrote, 'We also rejoice in our sufferings, because we know that suffering produces perseverance; perseverance, character; and character, hope. And hope does not disappoint us, because God has poured out his love into our hearts by the Holy Spirit, whom he has given us' (Romans 5:3–5). Christian hope strengthens us for the next hill and sees it as an opportunity for service and the development of a Christ-centred life.

Hills are shared, not solo challenges

Hills can be shared, not solo, challenges. Although I do go mountain biking on my own, it is much more fun to go with others. As a bit of a mountain bike 'evangelist', I like to ride with anyone who wants to have a go. To enable my family to join me, we have purchased one of those 'tag along' cycles that joins to my bike and transforms it into a pivoting tandem. My daughter can now go out riding with me and pedal her way up hills, while helping her father at the same time (the six gears on her one wheel make this a real possibility). Even when I go riding with friends, I notice that the benefits outweigh any disadvantages. Cycling with others means that you can usually ride for longer. The dull parts of any journey can be enlivened by conversation and the shared expectation of the 'good bits' ahead. Most of all, the hills can be conquered by each person in turn, putting in the extra effort that motivates the 'pack'. Even when riding with my daughter, I can exhort her to put in a bit of extra effort when I'm feeling weary. That way, we get to the top together.

We have considered the place of community and mutual support in our journeys of faith. Although there are times when we have to take a portion of our pilgrimage alone (or at least it feels like that), even then it is good to share our inner struggles with others. It is very worthwhile seeking out those who can listen to us and so accompany us while we are in the midst of difficulty. The sense of achievement in reaching the top of the hill with another is also so much sweeter. Journeying together means that you can empathize with each other in your struggle. You can encourage a less experienced climber when they really have done well. The more experienced can take joy in seeing the sense of accomplishment in the first-timer. All together, it is a more enriching experience. If 'the Way' is created with hills and valleys, it is essential that we see them through the eyes of faith in Christ, as places where our character will be formed and our faith in Jesus can be shared.

Aiming for the mountain-top

There is something called a 'mountain-top experience'. Moses, Peter, James and John all experienced it. (For Moses' story, see Exodus 19:20; for the experience of Peter, James and John, see Mark 9:2–7.) The mountain-top experience is unforgettable and life-changing, but in order to experience it there is no escaping the need to climb. The climb will be experienced in different ways: physically, emotionally and almost always spiritually. It is not the end, though, but the means, and however difficult it is at the time, God awaits to inspire and overawe us. Every hill we tackle brings us closer to the final mountain-top. Every turn of the pedals, or step of the way, moves us closer to the final 'holy mountain'. As we tackle the hill, we can see further into the distance. We might even catch a glimpse of the mountain-top that awaits us. We can look back and see where we have come from, as well as looking forward to where God ultimately wants us to be. Between here and there are many more hills, but with each one climbed, our spiritual reserves of strength can increase rather than diminishing.

Paul, one of the great disciples of Jesus, knew that the prize was worth the struggle and that each hill was worth the effort: 'I do not consider myself yet to have taken hold of it. But one thing I do: forgetting what is behind and straining toward what is ahead, I press on toward the goal to win the prize for which God has called me heavenward in Christ Jesus' (Philippians 3:13–14).

It is not the time to give up, but to look up and see the future that is just about to begin. From the top of the next hill, you can see you're nearly home.

Notes

1   Gerard W. Hughes, *God, Where Are You?* DLT, 1997, p. 52.

2   Richard Bauckham, *Freedom to Choose*, Grove Books, 1991p. 3.

3   Dallas Willard, *The Divine Conspiracy*, Fount, 1998 p. 297.

4   Willard, *The Divine Conspiracy*, p. 303 (emphasis in original).

5   Willard, *The Divine Conspiracy*, p. 309.

6   Willard, *The Divine Conspiracy*, p. 311.

7   Quoted in Nigel McCulloch, *Barriers to Belief*, DLT, 1994, pp. 26–27.

8   For further reading on this subject see Lesslie Newbigin, *Proper Confidence: Faith, Doubt and Certainty in Christian Discipleship*, SPCK, 1995, pp. 16ff.

9   Quoted in Thomas G. Long and Cornelius Plantinga, eds., *Martin Luther, A Chorus of Witnesses*, Eerdmans, 1994, p. 114.

10 Quoted in Hugh T. Kerr and John M. Mulder, eds., *Conversions: The Christian Experience*, Eerdmans, 1989, p. 187.

11 Philip Yancey, *Reaching for the Invisible God*, Zondervan, p. 41.

12 The framework for the section that follows owes acknowledgment to Bruce Milne, *The Message of John*, IVP, 1993, pp. 302–308.

13 Malcolm Goldsmith and Martin Wharton, *Knowing Me, Knowing You: Exploring Personality Type and Temperament*, SPCK, 2004, p. 159.

14 Mike Starkey, *God, Sex and Generation X*, Triangle, 1997, pp. 31–37, entitled 'Loss of the Past'.

15 Mark Stibbe, *O Brave New Church—Rescuing the Addictive Culture*, DLT, 1995, p. 94 (out of print).

16 G. Bilezikian, *Community 101*, Zondervan, 1997, p. 52.

17 P. Richter and L.J. Francis, *Gone but Not Forgotten*, DLT, 1998; M.J. Fanstone, *The Sheep That Got Away*, Monarch, 1993; P. Brierley, *The Tide is Running Out*, Christian Research, 2000.

18 J. Colwill, unpublished research entitled 'The Eutychus Project—Dropping In, Dropping Off, and Dropping Out: Church Leaving and Why it Happens'.

19 D. Tidball, *Skilful Shepherds*, IVP, 1997, p. 249.

20 N.T. Wright, *The New Testament and the People of God*, SPCK, 1992, p. 123.

21 S. Sunquist writes in *Dictionary of the Later New Testament* (IVP, p. 1151), 'Thus traditions have Thomas going to south India, north India and Parthis, but all traditions have him going to Asia and dying in Asia. Indian Christians mark his grave Mylapore, south of Madras in southeast India.'

22 William T. McLeod (ed.), *The Collins Paperback English Dictionary*, Collins.

23 Bauckham, *Freedom to Choose*, p. 9.

24 This search was carried out in January 2005. Similar searches carried out in subsequent months will lead to wildly differing results!

25 Matt Redman and others have made this the focus of their songwriting.

26 N.T. Wright, *Quiet Moments*, Lion Hudson, 2003, p. 3.

27 John Ortberg, *The Life You've Always Wanted*, Zondervan, 2004, pp. 76–77.

28 Nicky Gumbel, *Questions of Life*, Kingsway, 2003, pp. 195–196.

29 Statistics from www.cbnnews.com.

30 William Temple, *Readings in John's Gospel*, Macmillan, p. 28. Written in the days before inclusive language and first published in 1939, I believe we can infer that the word 'man' here includes all persons.

31 D.A. Carson, *The Gospel According to John*, IVP, 1991, p. 435.

32 F. Luke Wiseman, *Charles Wesley. Evangelist and Poet*, Epworth Press, 1933, p. 26 (out of print).

33 F.L. Cross and E.A. Livingstone (eds), *The Oxford Dictionary of the Christian Church*, OUP, 2005, p. 1466.

34 Winston Churchill, 'Blood, Toil, Tears, and Sweat', 13 May 1940.

35 See www.request.org.uk/main/history/laing/laing02.htm

36 Though not published in written form, John Ortberg's sermon 'Decision Time' has had a significant impact of the shape of this chapter. Contact WCA UK, PO Box 966, Southampton, England, SO15 2WT to listen to the tape of that sermon.

37 Willard, *The Divine Conspiracy*, p. 331.

38 Dietrich Bonhoeffer, *The Cost of Discipleship*, SCM, 2001, p. 27.

39 Bonhoeffer, *The Cost of Discipleship*, p. 29.

40 Bonhoeffer, *The Cost of Discipleship*, p. 38.

41 Bonhoeffer, *The Cost of Discipleship*, p. 43.

42 Dietrich Bonhoeffer, *Letters and Papers from Prison*, SCM, 2001 (latest edn.).

43 Eberhard Bethge, *Bonhoeffer, An Illustrated Biography*, Fount, 1995, p. 80.

44 Richard J. Foster and James Bryan Smith (eds), *Devotional Classics*, Hodder & Stoughton, 1993, p. 16.

45 A good place to start is any introductory section to a commentary on John's Gospel, where these matters will be discussed. Alternatively, theological dictionaries like *The Dictionary of Jesus and the Gospels* (IVP, 1992) are an option.

46 McLeod, *Collins English Dictionary.*

47 This proposal, though plausible on one level, does not take into account the way that in other passages Matthew's Gospel paints the disciples in a less than holy light. If that is true for Matthew 19:13, Matthew 16:22 and elsewhere, why should Matthew be seeking to cover something up on this occasion? Could it not be true that James and John's mother also made the request on a separate occasion?

48 *Wall Street* (1987) directed by Oliver Stone, Distributed by 20th Century Fox.

49 James was beheaded by Herod Agrippa around AD44.

50 For more information about the great work that Yeldall Manor do, go to www.yeldall.org.uk.

51 A book that has been a helpful guide through the subject of discipleship and dependency is Stibbe, *O Brave New Church—*

Rescuing the Addictive Culture. While I was at college, his lectures on John's Gospel and Mary Magdalene were equally inspirational.

52 Statistics drawn from *The Observer Magazine*, 18 February 2001

53 Stibbe, *O Brave New Church*, p. 6.

54 M.J. Wilkins, 'Disciples' in J.B. Green and S. McKnight (eds.), *Dictionary of Jesus and the Gospels*, p. 177.

55 Three recent examples are *The Last Temptation of Christ*, *Jesus of Montreal* and *The Passion of the Christ*.

56 Paul Fiddes, *Participating in God—A Pastoral Doctrine of the Trinity*, DLT, 2000, p. 36.

57 The Athanasian Creed, from *New Patterns for Worship. Creeds and Authorized Affirmations of Faith*, CHP, 2002

58 James M. Houston, *The Holy Spirit in Contemporary Spirituality*, Grove Books, 1993, p. 15.

59 David. S. Cunningham, *These Three are One: The Practice of Trinitarian Theology*, Challenges in Contemporary Theology series, Blackwell, 1997, p. 8.

60 John Ortberg, *If You Want to Walk on Water, You've Got to Get Out of the Boat*, Zondervan, 2001, pp. 77–78.

61 Anonymous Confederate soldier, American Civil War.

62 Kevin Adams, *A Diary of Revival*, CWR Publishing, 2004.

63 Carson, *Gospel According to John*, p. 678.

Resourcing your spiritual journey

through...

- Bible reading notes
- Books for Advent & Lent
- Books for Bible study and prayer
- Books to resource those working with under 11s in school, church and at home

- Quiet days and retreats
- Training for primary teachers and children's leaders
- Godly Play
- Barnabas Live

For more information, visit the **brf** website at **www.brf.org.uk**